Sweeney Todd

Anonymous

Level 3

Retold by Nancy Taylor

Series Editors: Andy Hopkins and Jocelyn Potter

Pearson Education Limited

Edinburgh Gate, Harlow,
Essex CM20 2JE, England
and Associated Companies throughout the world.

ISBN: 978-1-4479-6761-3

This edition first published by Pearson Education Ltd 2010

5 7 9 10 8 6 4

Text copyright © Pearson Education Ltd 2010

Illustrations by Alexander Jansson, c/o Shannon Associates

The moral rights of the authors have been asserted in accordance
with the Copyright Designs and Patents Act 1988

Set in 11/13pt A. Garamond
Printed in China
SWTC/04

Published by Pearson Education Ltd

Acknowledgements

We are grateful to the following for permission to reproduce photographs:

(Key: b-bottom; c-centre; l-left; r-right; t-top)

iStockphoto: Dave White 74r; Jupiter Unlimited: AbleStock.com 74c; Stockxpert 74l

All other images © Pearson Education

Every effort has been made to trace the copyright holders and we apologise in advance for any unintentional omissions.
We would be pleased to insert the appropriate acknowledgement in any subsequent edition of this publication.

For a complete list of the titles available in the Pearson English Active Readers series, visit www.pearsonenglishactivereaders.com.
Alternatively, write to your local Pearson Education office or to
Pearson English Readers Marketing Department, Pearson Education, Edinburgh Gate, Harlow, Essex CM20 2JE, England.

1.1 What's the book about?

1 Look at the pictures on the cover and on page 1. Circle the words that match your idea of the story.

   a   modern / old

   b   frightening / funny

   c   a love story / a murder mystery

   d   about a strange man / about an ordinary man

   e   in England / in the United States

2 Sweeney Todd and Johanna Oakley are both important to the story. Look at the pictures below and describe them. What do you imagine that they are like as people?

1.2 What happens first?

What do you think? Are these sentences right (✓) or wrong (✗)?

1 ☐ Sweeney Todd has a lot of good friends.

2 ☐ Sweeney Todd's shop is at the centre of a mystery.

3 ☐ Sweeney Todd is a kind, honest employer.

4 ☐ Sweeney Todd has many secrets.

5 ☐ Sweeney Todd is afraid of his neighbours and his customers.

Contents

CHAPTER 1

Two Exciting Days in 1785

Sweeney Todd was clearly unusual; perhaps he was even a little crazy.
But he had a successful business, so his neighbours accepted him.

Many years ago when George III was King of England, the area around Fleet Street was like many other busy parts of London. There was an old church, St Dunstan's, and many small houses and shops were crowded into the narrow streets.

One of the shops near the church was a small **barber**'s shop. The barber was a man with the unusual name of Sweeney Todd. This name was written in fat yellow letters above a little poem in the window:

Looking for a smooth face and tidy hair?
Take a seat in Sweeney Todd the barber's chair.

And what did this barber look like? He was a tall, ugly man with a very large mouth and unusually big hands and feet. And for a barber, he had terrible hair. It was very long, thick and untidy. Mr Sweeney Todd kept most of his barber's tools in his hair, but he kept his **razors** in his sitting-room. Nobody except Mr Todd went into this private room. The sitting-room and barber's shop were on the ground floor of the barber's very large house. The neighbours noticed that the upstairs rooms showed no signs of use.

barber /ˈbɑːbə/ (n) a man who cuts men's hair. He also shaves men's beards.
razor /ˈreɪzə/ (n) a sharp tool for shaving beards

1

The barber was also known for his unusually loud, frightening laugh. It was specially strange because he often seemed to laugh for no reason. Perhaps he was remembering a very funny personal story or joke.

Sweeney Todd was clearly unusual; perhaps he was even a little crazy. But he had a successful business, so his neighbours accepted him. They chose to forget about his strange hair, his frightening laugh and his big empty house. They went to him for a shave or a haircut, but they didn't become too friendly with him.

◆

'Listen carefully, Tobias Ragg,' began Sweeney Todd one rainy evening. 'I've given you a good job here, and you can learn a lot from me. One day you'll have a good profession as a barber. You have every reason to be a happy boy.'

Tobias was Sweeney Todd's only employee. The poor young boy worked long hours for a few pennies and was afraid of his employer.

'But remember my orders!' continued the barber. 'If you talk about me or my business, I will kill you. You don't ask questions. You don't think. You don't talk. Do you understand?'

'Yes, sir. I won't say anything. I promise. If I break my promise, you can give me to Mrs Lovett's for one of her meat **pies**.'

Sweeney Todd was a bit surprised by this suggestion. He looked carefully at the boy for a minute or two in silence. Then he said, 'Very good. Just remember that I can make very serious trouble for your mother. Now, run out and look at St Dunstan's clock. Find out the time.'

At the church Tobias learned that it was fifteen minutes to seven. On his way back to the barber's shop, he noticed a man with a dog looking at the clock too. But he couldn't think about them. He had to worry about Mr Todd's orders.

◆

'Almost seven o'clock, Hector,' the man in front of the church said to his dog. 'There's a barber's shop opposite. Perhaps I'll have a shave before I visit poor Miss Oakley. I have to tell her that Mark Ingestrie is dead. On the ship, his one subject of conversation was Miss Oakley: her beautiful eyes, her pretty mouth, her shiny hair. Now he's at the bottom of the Indian Ocean, and I have to give her this **pearl necklace**. Her heart will break because her true love is lost. But these pearls will make her rich. So I'll go for a shave immediately.'

The stranger crossed the street and went into Sweeney Todd's shop with his dog. 'I'd like a shave,' he said to the barber.

---

pie /paɪ/ (n) a food made of meat, fish, vegetables or fruit cooked in an oven
pearl /pɜːl/ (n) an expensive white round thing formed inside a sea animal
necklace /ˈnekləs/ (n) something that women wear around their necks

The man's dog **growled** softly and looked round. He lifted his head and smelled the air.

'Hector, what's wrong?' the man asked his dog. 'I've never seen you act like this before.'

'I have a fear of dogs, sir,' said Sweeney Todd. 'Please take him outside before he attacks me.'

'Hector doesn't attack without a reason,' said the man. 'But perhaps he doesn't like the look of you. I can understand that.'

When Hector was outside, he watched the door unhappily. He sensed that something inside the shop was not right.

'Tobias,' said Sweeney Todd before he began to shave his customer, 'go to Mr Peterson's shop and buy a bag of his little cakes for me.'

With the boy out of the shop, the barber began to talk to his customer. 'Where are you from, sir? What's your business in this part of the city?'

'I'm looking for a young woman named Johanna Oakley in Fore Street. Do you know her? Her father makes glasses for people who have problems with their eyes.'

'Yes, of course. She's a beautiful young lady. Are you a friend of hers?'

'No, sir, I've never met her. I'm a stranger here,' replied the customer. 'I've just returned from a journey to the Indian Ocean. My friend, Mark Ingestrie, went down with our ship, but he wanted Miss Oakley to have this fine pearl necklace.' He took it from his pocket and showed it to the barber. 'I'm going to give it to her after I have my shave.'

'Beautiful,' said Sweeney Todd, looking greedily at the pearls. 'Sir, I need a stronger razor for your thick beard. I'll return in one minute.'

Sweeney Todd walked into his sitting-room and closed the door. Suddenly there was a loud noise. Then the barber returned to his shop and walked to the empty chair. He picked up the customer's hat and quickly hid it in his cupboard.

◆

'Hello,' said Tobias, opening the door. 'I heard a terrible noise. Is everything all right? I forgot the money for the cakes.'

Sweeney Todd caught the boy's arm and pushed him against the wall.

'Speak!' cried Sweeney Todd. 'Speak or you die! How long were you watching at the door before you came in?'

'Watching? I wasn't watching anything, sir. I forgot the money for the cakes,' Tobias said, shaking with fear.

Sweeney Todd gave one of his frightening laughs and said, 'No, of course not. I was joking. Why don't you laugh at my joke?'

Tobias couldn't answer this question, but the barber quickly forgot about it.

growl /graʊl/ (v) to make a deep, angry sound

'What's that noise at my door?' he asked.

Tobias hurried to open the door. He found Hector there.

'It's that customer's dog, Mr Todd. It's strange that he didn't leave with his owner,' said Tobias.

'I hate dogs,' shouted the barber. 'Throw him into the street.'

But Hector ran quickly past the man and the boy and went straight to Mr Todd's cupboard.

'Stop him! Stop that **wicked** animal! Get him out of my shop!'

Hector was opening the cupboard door, and Sweeney Todd tried to pull him away. The dog turned suddenly and bit the barber's leg. Then he found his owner's hat and quickly ran out of the shop with it between his teeth.

'That's strange, isn't it, sir? Customers don't usually forget their hats and their dogs, do they?' said Tobias.

'Be quiet,' said Sweeney Todd. 'Here's old Mr Grant for his usual shave. Mr Grant, how pleasant to see you. Please sit down.'

'Yes, Todd. Any news today?'

wicked /'wɪkɪd/ (adj) acting in a way that is very wrong

'Nothing to report, sir,' said the barber. 'We haven't had a customer for almost two hours.'

'Sir, have you forgotten the man who left his hat and dog here?' began Tobias.

'Now I remember,' said Sweeney Todd angrily. 'After he left here I saw him in a fight at the corner of the market.'

'That's strange,' continued Tobias. 'I didn't see him on my way back from Mr Peterson's.'

'Tobias, please help me in the sitting-room for a minute.'

Todd threw the boy against the sitting-room wall and hit and kicked him. Then he locked the door of the room and returned to Mr Grant.

'I've given the boy some work to do in my office,' Sweeney Todd said. 'I'm sorry to keep you waiting.'

◆

'Johanna! Johanna!' shouted Mr John Oakley a day later, in Fore Street. 'My dear, your mother has gone to church and I haven't had any breakfast. Can you help me? I must open the shop soon. People are waiting for their glasses.'

Almost immediately Mr Oakley heard his only daughter's sweet voice. 'I'm coming, Father. I'll be down in two minutes.'

The girl hurried into the kitchen. She was eighteen years old but looked younger. Her shiny black hair was lovely next to her bright blue eyes and healthy skin. She spoke softly, but perhaps a little sadly, to her father.

'Please forgive me, Father. You had to wait for your breakfast.' She gave her father a quick kiss and began to prepare his morning meal.

'Dear Johanna, I'm sorry to worry you about my food. I have a lot of work in the shop, and your mother is always at church these days. There's a special meeting at St Dunstan's today because it is the twentieth of August. I don't understand it, but that church has become everything to your mother.'

'The twentieth of August,' Johanna said quietly. Then she fell into a chair and began to cry. She tried to stop her tears, but she couldn't. 'This date has made me late, Father.'

Old Mr Oakley looked nervously at his daughter. He loved her more than anything in the world. But how could he help her?

'Dear daughter,' he finally began, 'what's happened? Tell me or you will kill me with worry.'

'Father, I've tried to keep my secret, but I must tell you. You're always so kind and loving towards me, but your love cannot solve my problem. It cannot bring Mark Ingestrie back from the next world.'

'The young man is dead? How do you know? Why does this make you so unhappy? I didn't know that he was an important person in your life.'

'Father, I loved him and he loved me. We planned to marry. But first, he left here – two years ago – to make his **fortune**. He promised to return today, the twentieth day of August, 1785.'

'Johanna, why did you keep this secret from me?'

'Father, you believed that Mark Ingestrie was not a serious man. He had no money and he didn't have a profession. But he's a good man. He went to India to make money. He planned to return and begin a business here – for us, and our life together. Father, don't judge him badly. If you ever meet him again, you'll believe his words.'

'But you said that he's dead.'

'He promised to return today,' said the girl.

'And there are many more hours in this day,' her father told her.

'But I had a terrible dream last night,' began Johanna. 'I was sitting on a beach. The sea was rough and the waves were very high. The wind grew stronger and stronger. Far out at sea, I saw a ship. It was fighting against the wind and the waves, but it was losing the fight. The storm grew worse every second. Father, I was sure that Mark Ingestrie was on that ship. But I sat on the sand and could do nothing. Finally I heard a loud cry and watched the ship disappear under the waves. All was lost and the world was silent again. I tried to

fortune /ˈfɔːtʃən/ (n) a lot of money

scream, but no sound came from my mouth.

'Then I saw something in the water. It was a man holding on to a piece of wood from the ship. I knew it was him – Mark Ingestrie.'

'But, Johanna, you cannot believe in a dream,' cried Mr Oakley.

'Father, he called my name, but I couldn't move. I couldn't save him. He fought against the waves, and then I saw him go under the water. He was gone.'

'You didn't see this, Johanna. You dreamed it. It wasn't real. And Mark Ingestrie hasn't returned with a fortune. Now dry your eyes and forget about him. But tell me the name of his ship, and I'll ask about it and about him. Don't believe that he's dead. Men like him often surprise us. But why didn't he stay in London and work hard here?'

Her father's words seemed unkind, but Johanna heard the sound of his loving voice. He always understood her feelings and was always kind to her.

◆

That same morning a ship from India sat at a seaport not far from London. When the sun came up, the seamen were already awake. The **captain** of the ship was watching the beach. He was looking carefully for something or someone.

'Where is Mr Thornhill? Have you got any ideas?' The captain was talking to Mr Jeffery, the officer standing next to him. 'He went into the city last night to do some business at Temple Gate near Fleet Street. But why hasn't he returned? It's unusual for him to be away from the ship.'

'He's coming now,' said Mr Jeffery, a good friend of Mr Thornhill. 'You'll see him in a few minutes.'

'How do you know that?' asked the captain.

'Because I can see his dog. Look! He's swimming towards the ship.'

'Why is that dog in the water?' asked the captain. 'Why isn't he in a boat with Mr Thornhill? Something's wrong here. The dog looks very tired, and he's carrying a hat in his mouth. Help him on to the ship!'

The dog fell to the floor when the men pulled him out of the water. But he still held Mr Thornhill's hat tightly between his teeth.

'This worries me,' said the captain. 'What can this mean? A dog, a hat, but no Thornhill.'

Hector was popular with the men on the ship. They soon gave him food and water and tried to make him comfortable. But the dog couldn't rest. He pulled at the captain's coat, trying to move him towards the beach.

'Look at him!' cried the captain. 'He wants me to follow him. I'm sure that Thornhill's in trouble.'

captain /ˈkæptn/ (n) the most important officer on a ship

The captain and Mr Jeffery called for a boat and sailed up the River Thames with the dog towards Temple Gate. It was still very early, so they quickly arrived at the old Temple steps. Hector immediately jumped out of the boat. He ran towards Fleet Street with the two men following closely behind. Finally the dog stopped outside Sweeney Todd's shop. He sat down and growled at the barber's door.

The door of the shop opened suddenly. Mr Todd tried to hit the dog with a heavy metal bar, but Hector was too quick for him.

'What was that? Why did the barber come out and try to kill Hector?' asked Mr Jeffery. 'Something strange is happening here.'

The men knocked on Sweeney Todd's door, but he refused to come outside. 'I won't open the door if that dog's there,' he shouted. 'He's crazy or hates me for no reason.'

'I'll hold the dog,' said the captain. 'He won't hurt you.'

Finally Sweeney Todd opened the door and calmly said, 'Good day, sirs. What do you need – a shave or a haircut?'

'Neither, sir,' said the captain. 'We're looking for our friend, the owner of this dog. He's a very intelligent dog, and he's brought us here. We believe that our friend was here yesterday evening.'

'Excuse me for a minute, please,' said the barber. 'Tobias! Run to Mr Philip's shop and get me some apples. And don't forget to take the money this time. Now, go!'

When Tobias was out of the shop, Sweeney Todd turned to the captain and Mr Jeffery. 'Tell me again. How can I help you?'

'Did a man from our ship visit your shop yesterday evening?' the captain asked.

'A tall, handsome man with bright blue eyes and fair hair?' asked Sweeney Todd.

'Yes, yes! That's him!' said Mr Jeffery.

'Yes, he was here. I shaved him and gave him a fine finish.'

'What do you mean by a fine finish?' asked Mr Jeffery.

'I did my job. I made him look tidy, like a businessman with an important meeting. Then I told him how to get to Fore Street. After he left, I saw him fighting with another man near the market.'

'Was this dog with him?' the captain asked.

'There was a dog, but not inside my shop,' said Sweeney Todd.

'But it's strange that the dog brought us here. Surely it means that he lost Thornhill here,' said the captain.

'Or perhaps on Fore Street,' suggested Sweeney Todd. 'Your friend was looking for a girl called Oakley. Her father has a shop on that street. He makes glasses.'

'That's right,' said Mr Jeffery. 'Mr Thornhill had something to give Miss Oakley. Something very expensive. How do we get to Fore Street from here?'

The captain and Mr Jeffery left the shop, but Hector refused to move. He sat at the barber's door with Mr Thornhill's hat next to him. A small crowd of people stood near the dog, hoping to see some excitement. Hector looked sad, sitting on the street with the hat at his side. Some people even threw money into it.

Sweeney Todd watched the dog and became angrier and angrier. At the same time, he was afraid of the dog and afraid to leave the shop. But finally, with a long knife in his hand, he walked out of his door. Surprisingly, the dog didn't attack him, but he looked up at Sweeney Todd with sad eyes. Hector couldn't speak, but his meaning was clear. He seemed to say, 'Where is Mr Thornhill, the best owner in the world? Give him back to me, and I'll forgive you.'

'Where's the dog's owner?' shouted a man in the crowd.

'He's probably dead,' said Sweeney Todd.

'The dog says you killed him,' said another. 'What do you say?' The crowd laughed.

'The dog is wrong,' Sweeney Todd said. He didn't want to discuss Mr Thornhill with these people. He turned and hurried back inside his shop. But when he sat down, he was smiling. What wicked plan was forming in his dark mind?

2.1 Were you right?

Look back at your answers to Activity 1.2 on page iv. Then read the sentences below and imagine what will happen. Circle a or b.

1 Some people in Fleet Street are planning a party.

   a Sweeney Todd is the first person that they invite.

   b They don't invite Sweeney Todd.

2 Children play a game and one of them is Sweeney Todd.

   a That child is always laughing and full of fun.

   b That child tries to frighten his friends.

3 Tobias Ragg arrives late for work.

   a Sweeney Todd doesn't pay him for the morning.

   b Sweeney Todd asks about his health.

4 A customer asks Sweeney Todd about his personal history.

   a Sweeney Todd changes the subject of the conversation.

   b Sweeney Todd smiles and tells the man about his family.

5 A neighbour wants to use the barber's upstairs rooms.

   a The barber laughs at this request.

   b The barber feels nervous and hides from his neighbour.

2.2 What more did you learn?

Complete each sentence with names from Chapter 1. Then discuss the questions that follow.

1 .... acts badly towards ...., his only employee. (In what ways?)

2 Mr .... wants to find Miss .... (Why?)

3 .... hears Sweeney Todd lie to Mr .... about his last customer. (What are the two lies?)

4 .... has a frightening dream about the death of .... (Why on this day?)

5 .... takes Mr .... and others from the ship to Fleet Street. (Why?)

2.3 Language in use

Look at the sentences on the right.
Then complete these sentences with
past progressive forms of the verbs.

> 'How long **were** you **watching**
> at the door?'
>
> 'I **wasn't watching** anything, sir.'

1   While Sweeney Todd ....*was shaving*............. Mr Thornhill, the man's dog

.... outside and Tobias Ragg ....

to Mr Peterson's shop. (shave, sit, hurry)

2   On the morning of August 20th, Mr Oakley .... for his

breakfast, but his wife .... about him or his stomach.

(wait, think)

3   In Johanna Oakley's dream, Mark Ingestrie and the men on his ship

.... their fight against a terrible storm. (lose)

4   On the morning of August 20th, Mr Jeffery and his men ....

about their journey from India. They .... about Mr Thornhill.

(talk, worry)

5   Sweeney Todd's neighbours .... about Hector and his

owner, but the barber .... (joke, laugh)

2.4 What happens next?

What do you think? Draw a line between the people
(and one animal) and the questions that worry them.

Tobias Ragg   1   What can I do to find
                        my friend Thornhill?

Sweeney Todd   2   Will that barber come outside
                        with his metal bar again?

Hector   3   Is my mother a criminal?

Johanna Oakley   4   Will that boy stop asking questions about
                        my customers?

Mr Jeffery   5   Will there ever be any news about Mark Ingestrie?

11

CHAPTER 2

Missing Customers and a Disappearing Dog

People of every description – rich and poor, young and old, male and female –
wanted one of Mrs Lovett's pies for their lunch.

The people around Fleet Street always knew the time by looking at
St Dunstan's Church. Now the clock told them that it was twelve o'clock.
It was time for lunch. Suddenly office doors opened and groups of young
men hurried into the narrow streets. They talked and laughed as they pushed
through the crowds on their way to Bell Court. What was happening? Was
there a fire? Was there a fight? Why were these young men so excited?

There wasn't any serious trouble in the area. These men – and many others
too – were racing towards Bell Court because they wanted to be the first
customers of the day at Mrs Lovett's pie shop.

People of every description – rich and poor, young and old, male and
female – wanted one of Mrs Lovett's pies for their lunch. They were famous in
every corner of the city because they were the richest, the most **delicious** pies
in London. The taste of the meat and the fat in these pies was famous. In fact,
people often bought one and then almost immediately ordered another.

delicious /dɪˈlɪʃəs/ (adj) tasting very good

Without question, the pies were the best in the city. But the shop's customers also had one more reason for eating a meat pie at lunchtime: Mrs Lovett. The owner of the pie shop was quite young and quite pretty. She smiled at the young men, and suddenly they felt hungry for another pie. But some customers saw something different, something not so lovely, in Mrs Lovett. They noticed the smile on her face, but did it come from her heart? Was she hiding a wicked side? But they continued to buy more and more of her wonderful pies, and the fair Mrs Lovett grew richer and richer.

On this sunny afternoon Tobias Ragg was in the crowd in the pie shop, and he was in a hurry. 'One pie, please, Mrs Lovett,' he shouted.

'Tobias!' cried a young man with his mouth full of pie. 'I haven't seen you for months. Where are you working now?'

'Hello, Mr Clift. I'm with Sweeney Todd, the barber of Fleet Street, close to St Dunstan's Church.'

'That's interesting,' said Mr Clift. 'I'm going to a party tonight. I'll come and have a shave.'

Tobias put his mouth near his friend's ear and said quietly, 'Don't.'

Then the boy hurried back to the barber's shop. The dog with the hat was still outside. He spoke to the dog. 'Why are you here, boy? Are you hungry?'

Tobias gave the dog a piece of meat from his pocket, and then he heard another very loud noise from inside the shop. As he hurried inside, he saw a handsome walking stick with a gold top and an expensive hat on the table. The boy was also surprised to see an empty barber's chair. He didn't say a word when he saw his employer. Mr Todd came out of his sitting room, drying his hands. He looked uglier and more wicked than ever.

'Well, Tobias,' the barber said, 'you've had one of Mrs Lovett's delicious pies for lunch.'

'How does he know?' thought Tobias. 'Yes, sir,' he said. 'But I didn't stay a minute. Look, sir. Another customer has left his hat. And his walking stick. What shall I do with them?'

Without a word, Sweeney Todd lifted the walking stick and hit Tobias across his shoulders. The boy fell to the floor.

'Have you forgotten your lessons? You must not speak about my business. It's not *your* business, and it's not my neighbours' business. Think your thoughts, but don't speak about them to anybody.'

'Mr Todd, I'm your employee. You mustn't hit and kick me. I won't work here if you do. I'll find a different job,' Tobias said.

'My boy, have you forgotten about your mother?'

'You can't hurt my mother,' shouted Tobias.

'Is that right? I'll tell you a little story. Last winter the temperature was below freezing, and you and your mother had no food on the table and no money for the bills. Your mother solved this problem by stealing a small silver box from Mr King, her employer.

'Mr King is a customer of mine. If an employee steals from him, he calls the police. I protected your mother from Mr King last year. But I'll tell him about the silver box if you forget my lesson. Then the police will happily **hang** your mother. Remember that and keep your mouth shut.'

'Please, sir, I'll say nothing – I'll think nothing. Please don't hurt my mother. I'll work very hard for you,' Tobias promised seriously.

◆

In the house on Fore Street above Mr Oakley's shop, poor Johanna Oakley also felt serious, and very sad. The day was coming to an end, and she still had no news of Mark Ingestrie. Her steps were heavy as she climbed the stairs to her bedroom. She needed to be alone and to think about her missing **sweetheart**.

'Oh, Mark!' she cried as tears ran down her face. 'Have you forgotten me? Why haven't you sent me a word or a sign of your love?'

Johanna lay all night without sleeping. She remembered her dream and couldn't stop crying. 'He's dead. I know it!' she told herself.

But the sun came up in the morning, and with it there was a sign of hope. When Johanna looked out of her bedroom window, she saw a man in a doorway on the opposite side of the street. This stranger was watching the Oakley house very closely. He saw Johanna and politely lifted his hat. Then he threw something through her open bedroom window and quickly walked away.

Johanna's heart was racing as she picked up a small envelope. With shaking fingers she opened it and read the note inside. 'For news of Mark Ingestrie, come to the Temple Gardens one hour before the sun goes down. Don't be afraid. I'm a friend and will have a white rose in my hand.'

'Mark's alive! Nothing matters except this wonderful news!'

In the late afternoon Johanna walked happily towards her meeting. On the way she noticed a dog sitting outside the barber's shop on Fleet Street. The animal looked very sad. He was guarding a hat which lay next to him on the ground. As she looked at the dog, the door opened a little. A hand came out and threw a piece of meat towards the dog.

'Those kind people are worried about that poor dog,' Johanna said to herself. But the dog didn't eat the meat. Johanna looked more closely and saw something unusual on it. It looked like the white **poison** that her father

---

hang /hæŋ/ (v) to kill someone by hanging them from something by their neck
sweetheart /'swiːthɑːt/ (n) someone who you love in a romantic way
poison /'pɔɪzən/ (n) something that can kill you. After you eat it, you become very ill.

sometimes bought from the chemist.

Suddenly the door opened a little wider and Johanna saw the ugly face of Sweeney Todd. 'That terrible man is trying to poison that dog,' she thought. She felt afraid as she continued towards the Temple Gardens.

When she arrived at the gardens, Johanna was thinking about her lovely times with Mark Ingestrie two summers earlier. She awoke from her daydream when she saw a man with a white rose at the park gate.

'Excuse me, I believe you're Miss Johanna Oakley,' said the stranger.

'Yes, sir. And are you Mark Ingestrie's messenger?'

'Not exactly. May I introduce myself? My name is Mr Jeffery. I have news of Mr Ingestrie, but he hasn't sent me.'

'Sir, does that mean you have bad news? Please tell me immediately or my heart will break. Is he alive?'

'My message is very sad,' said Mr Jeffery. 'Remember that there are problems and accidents everywhere. A trip to India is always full of danger.'

'Don't say another word,' cried Johanna. 'My dream has come true. My life is finished. Mark! Mark! You have left me alone on this earth.'

'Please, miss, wait to hear my story from the beginning. I don't know if your sweetheart's alive. But I also cannot say that he's dead.'

'Is there still hope? Speak again!' Johanna said urgently.

'Be calm, please. He's *probably* dead. But you must listen carefully and decide.'

'Yes, yes! Tell me everything.'

'I, like Mr Ingestrie, was on a ship to India. Miss Oakley, do you understand the type of adventure that Mr Ingestrie began two years ago?'

'He went away to make his fortune. We wanted to marry, but he had no money and no profession,' Johanna explained.

'Yes, like many young men, he went to India to find his way in the world. But before Mr Ingestrie left London, he met a man. This man had a report about gold – lots of gold – on one of the small islands near the Indian seas. Mr Ingestrie decided to search for this gold and then return to England with a large fortune. But he needed money for a ship, equipment and men. Luckily a very rich man heard Ingestrie when he was talking about his dream. This older man believed in your sweetheart because he felt so sure of success in India. The rich man decided to pay for everything to send the younger man on his adventure. He believed they could both make a lot of money from the journey.'

'Were you on Mr Ingestrie's ship?' asked Johanna.

'No, I never saw him. I was told this story by a man who sailed with him. His name is Thornhill, and he was on Ingestrie's ship. They became very close friends during the trip. Thornhill planned to visit you yesterday with a message and a gift from your sweetheart. But something has happened to him. He didn't arrive at your house, and he didn't return to our ship. We're worried about him, and you're clearly worried about Mr Ingestrie.'

'This is good news! Mark Ingestrie has kept his promise to me. He tried to send a message to me on 20 August 1785. But what happened at sea? Can you tell me more?'

'There was a lot of work before Mr Ingestrie's ship, the *Star*, could leave England. But finally the adventure began, and your sweetheart and a group of brave men left for India. They were full of hope and very excited about their trip. The *Star* reached the Indian Ocean and the island with the gold.

'I saw the ship, on its return, when it was in the middle of the Indian Ocean. Sadly I watched it disappear under the waves. It was never seen again,' Mr Jeffery continued.

'Gone! Disappeared! This happened in my dream,' cried Johanna.

'Yes, the ship was gone, but I'll finish my story. I was on the *Neptune*, another British ship. We too were returning to England when we saw a big storm coming. It lasted for three nights and two days and carried us more than a hundred kilometres away. When the weather was finally calm again, we saw a fire on the water. After about half an hour, we got closer to the fire. We could see that . . . '

'It was his ship on fire!' guessed Johanna. 'The *Star*?'

'It was. We hurried, but we were still far away from the burning ship. There was nothing we could do. We had to watch the *Star* go down and see the water close over her forever.'

'Can you be sure that it was the *Star*?'

'Listen. We continued towards the place where the ship disappeared. We hoped to pick up some of the men. Our captain suddenly saw a man with a dog holding onto a piece of wood. It was Mr Thornhill, and we learned about Mark Ingestrie and the *Star* from him. We didn't find any other men.

'I became friends with Thornhill. He's intelligent, kind and amusing. I learned a lot about him and his life. Then one day he said, "I have a very sad job when I arrive in London. My best friend on the *Star* was Mark Ingestrie. He was a brave young man with many hopes and dreams. But he worried sometimes about returning to London alive. He wanted to be a success for his sweetheart, a girl named Johanna Oakley. He gave me a pearl necklace to keep safe for her. Now he's dead, and I must find her and give the necklace to her from him. It's the fortune that he left for her."

'When we reached the River Thames three days ago, Mr Thornhill left us. He and his dog went into the city to find you.'

'But he never came to my house!' cried Johanna.

'That's the mystery. His dog took us to a barber's shop in Fleet Street. Did Thornhill disappear from there? We don't know, but we haven't heard anything from him. We simply can't find him.'

'Is the barber called Sweeney Todd?' asked Johanna.

'Yes! And Thornhill's dog, Hector, refuses to leave his shop.'

'I saw that sad dog on my way here! And you say that his life is tied to mine! Oh! Mark! Are you dead or alive? Is there any hope for you? Are you lost forever?'

'We cannot know for sure, but he probably is dead. And now we must find Mr Thornhill and your pearls. Perhaps a thief saw them and killed Thornhill for them.'

'A pearl necklace means nothing to me,' cried Johanna.

Mr Jeffery looked at her sad face. 'Miss Oakley, this has been a terrible day for you. Can I please walk you to your door?'

Johanna felt grateful for Mr Jeffery's arm as they walked towards her home. As they passed the barber's shop, they were both surprised. The dog and the hat were gone.

◆

Mr Jeffery felt both worried and sad as he left Johanna Oakley near her home. Miss Oakley now knew Mark Ingestrie's story, but she didn't know about the later storms and dangers in the Indian Ocean. The *Neptune* had to face weeks of bad weather before she arrived back in England. During this difficult and dangerous journey, Mr Jeffery became close friends with Mr Thornhill. They worked together to repair the ship after the storms. They had a lot of time for long conversations, and a deep friendship grew between them. During these weeks they discovered many similar interests and discussed every subject under the sun. Their friendship gave the two men hope. They began to believe in a successful return to England.

One night, in the middle of the worst storm, Mr Jeffery almost went over the side of the ship. At the last possible minute, Mr Thornhill caught Jeffery's arm and saved his friend from death. This frightening adventure brought the two men even closer. Mr Jeffery was forever grateful to Mr Thornhill, and now here in London he had one clear purpose. He had to find Mr Thornhill. It was *his* turn to save his friend's life.

With this purpose in his mind, Mr Jeffery went to visit another old friend from his life at sea, Captain Rathbone. The older man welcomed Jeffery warmly and then the two friends discussed the problem. Mr Jeffery quickly explained the mystery of the disappearance of Mr Thornhill and his dog.

'Sir, I've come to ask for your help,' Jeffery explained.

'I'm not sure if I can help,' replied Captain Rathbone. 'But this is very interesting. It was a good idea to follow the dog to Fleet Street. Are you sure that Thornhill left the barber's shop after his shave?'

'Sweeney Todd, the barber, says that he left. He says that Thornhill went towards Fore Street. But first he was in a fight near the market.'

'But the dog took you to the barber's shop,' said Captain Rathbone. 'Is Mr Todd lying to you? We must discover more about this barber. I suggest that we go to his shop as customers tomorrow morning. Will he remember you from your first visit?'

'I don't think so. I was wearing my officer's clothes from the ship, and now I'm wearing an ordinary suit – and it was a very short visit.'

'We must find a way to bring the pearl necklace into our conversation with the barber. Did he see the necklace and rob Mr Thornhill? Is that what you're afraid of?' asked Captain Rathbone.

'The necklace is very **valuable**, but very difficult for a thief to sell. A buyer couldn't wear it openly. Where did it come from? Where was it bought? It will be difficult for a thief to find a buyer. How can we find out if Sweeney Todd has the pearl necklace?' asked Mr Jeffery.

'We'll go to the barber's shop as two men who sell **jewellery**. We'll ask for a shave and then talk about our business in the usual way of conversation. Is Sweeney Todd a thief? Perhaps a murderer? We'll watch him closely and decide,' Captain Rathbone suggested.

The next morning the two men walked down Fleet Street towards the little shop that was so full of mystery.

'You see,' said Mr Jeffery to Captain Rathbone, 'the dog's not here. I imagine that the barber has destroyed him.'

'Don't judge the man until we finish our examination. Businessmen don't want dogs sitting outside their shops. Perhaps Mr Todd is **innocent** and simply grew tired of the dog.'

'You're right. Let's find out when we talk to him. But remember – we won't say anything about Thornhill or his dog,' said Jeffery.

'I agree. This morning we're just two men in need of a shave.'

'Good morning, sirs,' Sweeney Todd greeted the two new detectives. 'Would you like shaves and haircuts?'

'Shaves only, please,' answered Captain Rathbone. 'We're in a hurry.'

'Please sit down,' said the barber. 'I'll soon finish yours and then shave your friend. Have you seen the newspaper this morning? There's a mysterious

valuable /ˈvæljuəbəl, -jəbəl/ (adj) costing a lot of money
jewellery /ˈdʒuːəlri/ (n) things made of gold, silver and valuable stones. You wear them around your neck, on your arms, in your ears or on your clothes.
innocent /ˈɪnəsənt/ (adj) not a criminal

business about a man named Fidler. He left his office yesterday afternoon to pick up a large amount of money from his bank. Nobody has seen him since then. His family and the police are worried about him. His secretary says that he was wearing a brown coat and carrying a very valuable walking stick with a gold top. Very strange, don't you agree?'

Mr Jeffery and Captain Rathbone heard a low sound coming from the corner of the room. 'What's that?' asked Mr Jeffery. 'Is there an animal in the corner?'

'Oh, it's only my assistant, Tobias Ragg. He's got a pain in his stomach because he eats too many of Mrs Lovett's famous meat pies. You must be more careful, boy,' shouted Sweeney Todd.

'Yes, sir,' said Tobias quietly. But then he made a painful noise again, and his eyes filled with tears.

Captain Rathbone was finished, and now Mr Jeffery sat in the barber's chair.

'Be quick, Mr Green,' Captain Rathbone said to Mr Jeffery. 'We have an important meeting with the prince. We don't want to lose our big sale today.'

'You're right. We sat for too long at the breakfast table. But you know that the prince loves special jewellery. He'll pay a high price for things that he really likes.'

'So, you sell jewellery?' asked Sweeney Todd. 'That sounds better than shaving beards.'

'I think it probably is,' said Mr Jeffery. 'And possibly there's more money in our business.'

'I've worked in this shop for many years,' said the barber. 'Finally I've saved enough money to leave London. I'm planning a quiet life in the country. And, there you are, sir, shaved and clean, and all for one penny.'

Jeffery and Rathbone wanted to find out more about Sweeney Todd, but their business with him was finished.

The barber watched as the two men walked down Fleet Street. 'Clever – very intelligent and very careful – but I'm not so stupid. Of course they weren't jewellery sellers. They probably have an interest in one special pearl necklace. Luckily I don't believe everything my customers say. Isn't that right, Tobias?'

'Yes, sir,' said the boy quietly.

'And never forget my orders, boy. Your mother will hang if you ever tell those two men – or anybody – about me or my business.'

◆

'That didn't help us,' said Mr Jeffery to Captain Rathbone. 'He's either too clever for us or he's innocent.'

'I can't believe that he's innocent,' said Captain Rathbone. 'His face changed when we talked about the prince and expensive jewellery. And clearly the boy's afraid of him. Look! Isn't that him – the barber's boy? He looks almost ill with worry.'

The men called to Tobias.

'My boy,' began Mr Jeffery, 'does the barber make you so unhappy and worried?'

'No, no, I've got nothing to tell. Let me pass, please,' cried Tobias.

'Why are you so nervous? We won't hurt you. We'll give you a pound if you answer our questions,' Captain Rathbone continued. 'What happened to the owner of the dog? The dog with the hat?'

'Nothing! Nothing to say,' cried Tobias.

'We'll protect you from Mr Todd,' Mr Jeffery said very kindly. 'Please help us. Did you see our friend in the barber's shop?'

'He was shaved and he left. That's all.'

'But why did the dog stay at the shop?' asked the captain.

'I know nothing. Don't keep me here. Oh, my poor mother . . . '

'Boy, we want to help you. Don't keep Mr Todd's dangerous secrets. We'll get you away from him and protect you,' promised Mr Jeffery.

'No! Nothing to say.'

Both men were sure that Tobias had a lot to say about Mr Todd and about Mr Thornhill. But the boy refused to speak against his employer. Jeffery and Rathbone left Fleet Street with no new information about Thornhill. And was Sweeney Todd an innocent man? Possibly, but not in the opinion of those two men.

3.1 Were you right?

Look back at your answers to Activity 2.4. Then explain what you know about these people and things.

1 Tobias Ragg's mother and Mr King's silver box

2 A customer's handsome walking stick and hat and a hit across the shoulders for Tobias

3 Meat with poison on it and Hector

4 An envelope through Johanna Oakley's window and Mark Ingestrie

5 Mr Jeffery and Captain Rathbone

3.2 What more did you learn?

Write the names. Who . . .

1 is the owner of a very successful pie shop? ....

2 tells Mr Clift to stay away from Sweeney Todd's barber shop? ....

3 carries a white rose to the Temple Gardens? ....

4 disappeared when the *Star* went under the waves? ....

5 saved Mr Jeffery's life during a terrible storm? ....

6 disappears after a trip to the bank? ....

7 like Jeffery, acts the part of a jewellery seller? ....

8 thinks Mr Jeffery and Captain Rathbone are clever actors? ....

3.3 Language in use

Look at the sentences on the right. Then complete the sentences below. Use the present perfect forms of these verbs:

> 'Another customer **has left** his hat.'
>
> 'Why **haven't** you **sent** me a word or a sign of your love?'

| ask | eat | try | sleep | discover | have |

1 Mrs Lovett's customers

....

a lot of pies today.

2 Tobias and his mother

....

an easy life.

3 Johanna

....

all night.

4 The barber

....

to kill Hector again.

5 Mr Jeffery

....

Captain Rathbone for help.

6 The two detectives

....

anything about Thornhill yet.

3.4 What happens next?

Discuss possible ways to finish these sentences.

1 Mrs Lovett's only employee is unhappy because . . .

2 Johanna wants to talk to her best friend because . . .

3 Johanna and Mr Jeffery have a second meeting because . . .

4 Sweeney Todd takes a trip outside London with a pearl necklace in his pocket because . . .

5 Tobias runs away from Sweeney Todd's shop because . . .

CHAPTER 3

A Time for Making Plans

Suddenly Tobias jumped to his feet. He had a plan! 'Todd won't return for quite a long time. I'm going to search this house and discover his wicked secrets.'

It was late. Mrs Lovett was ready to close the pie shop for the night. But before she could lock the door, a very thin, poor-looking young man came into the shop. He started to speak, but Mrs Lovett stopped him.

'Go away!' she said in her most unfriendly voice. 'I never give my pies to people who have no money. If you can't pay, you don't eat here.'

The young man looked angry for a few seconds, but he answered politely. 'Mrs Lovett, I'm not asking for a free pie. I'm looking for a job. Do you need anybody to work in your shop?'

'Why do you think I'll give *you* a job? You're dirty and you smell bad.'

'I've had some terrible times, but in the past I was one of your best customers. I enjoyed your pies and your smiles, but now I have nothing. I'm a broken man, and I'll take any job. Please help me. I'm so hungry. I've got nothing and nobody,' the young man explained.

'An interesting story, but that's your business, not mine. With my pie man in the **cellar** and me in the shop, there's no job for you here.'

'Thank you for your time,' the poor young man said politely but very sadly.

But before he could open the door, Mrs Lovett had an idea. Her pie man was becoming difficult – he wanted to leave the cellar. Perhaps she did need a new employee.

cellar /ˈselə/ (n) a room under a house or building

'Come back in two hours,' she told the young man at her door. 'And take a pie with you now.'

The man was so pleased! 'My name's Jarvis Williams, Mrs Lovett. I'll be back in exactly two hours. And thank you for the pie. It's delicious!'

When Mrs Lovett was alone, she spoke to herself in a strange, low voice. 'He'll suit me for a few months. Most of the men are useful for a month or two. But first I need to finish with that stupid pie man in the cellar.'

◆

Mrs Lovett's cellar covered a large area under Bell Court and Fleet Street. It was a dark, lonely place with a big oven and lots of shelves along the walls for the pie man's tools and the pie **trays**. The shelves on the opposite side of the large cellar held the meat and other things that went into the famous pies. These arrived mysteriously through hidden doors in the walls.

The pie man had to work very hard, producing thousands of pies every day, for the shop and for hundreds of customers around London. As a result of all this business, Mrs Lovett was growing rich, but her pie men always grew more and more unhappy. They lived alone in the dark cellar and began to dream of the world above them. But none of the pie men ever left the cellar alive. Of course Mrs Lovett never told this fact to new employees.

Mrs Lovett's present pie man, Mr Skinner, was very tired of his life in the cellar. He was lonely, and he was sick of Mrs Lovett's pies. In fact, the *idea* of Mrs Lovett's pies made him ill. He sat on his hard chair and looked at the great dark, empty space around him.

'I must leave tonight,' he told himself. 'I know Mrs Lovett's secrets, and my head is full of terrible pictures. I haven't slept for five nights, and I can't eat another pie. I must find a way out. I must see the streets and smell fresh air and eat healthy food. But what's that noise?'

Mr Skinner stood up and listened, but everything was quiet again except the oven. 'I've been here for six weeks and my heart has died inside me. Why is the door locked? How can I leave this terrible prison?'

'Skinner!' Mrs Lovett shouted through a small window above him. 'When will you finish the cooking for tonight?'

'In fifteen minutes,' Mr Skinner answered quietly.

The window above him closed, and the pie man was alone again. He began to think of his early days as a young, happy child. He imagined green trees, a beautiful river, bird-song, good friends, games, a happy home.

'Why am I thinking about the past tonight? I can clearly imagine my friends and family. They seem to be waiting for me. But how can I reach them?'

tray /treɪ/ (n) a flat piece of plastic, wood or metal used for carrying plates and food

Mr Skinner was lost in his dreams and didn't notice activity behind him. A small door opened and a man came into the cellar. He walked silently to the pie man's chair. Then he lifted a heavy metal bar slowly over his head. The bar came down quickly. Before he could scream, Mr Skinner's head was broken into two tidy pieces. Perhaps he really did see his dead parents that night.

'Mr Jarvis Williams, I see that you can tell the time,' said Mrs Lovett. The tired, thin man was waiting at her door.

'Yes, Mrs Lovett, and I hope you have good news for me. Nobody will give me a job after my difficult times. I look so terrible, and I'm so poor and hungry.'

'Well, if you have the right skills, you'll be a good pie man. Follow me and I'll show you the cellar. You can eat pies all day, but I won't give you any other food or any money. And you cannot leave the cellar.'

'What? I can never leave? I don't understand,' said Mr Williams.

'Of course you can leave. I don't keep people if they aren't comfortable here.

But you can leave only once. You cannot come back. If you agree to that, you can have the job,' explained Mrs Lovett.

'But what happened to your other pie man?' asked the young man. 'He's gone to visit some of his oldest friends. He won't return. Do you want the job?'

'Yes, yes!' shouted Mr Williams. 'I'm ready to work. Thank you for the job and the food and a place to live. You're very kind.'

Mr Jarvis Williams followed Mrs Lovett through a number of doors and down many stairs into the dark cellar. She showed him the tools, trays and meat, and explained his work.

'Where does the meat come from? Who puts it on the shelf?' asked the young man.

'That's not your business. You must follow my orders and make the pies on time every day. That's *your* job,' said Mrs Lovett coldly.

Then she showed the new pie man how to make the pies quickly and easily. She explained about the oven. She told him to put the fresh pies on the large trays and to send them up to the shop on a special lift. In the roof of the cellar there was a large door. It opened when the pies arrived there. Then Mrs Lovett had a big tray of fresh pies for her customers in the shop above.

'And now I must leave you,' said Mrs Lovett. 'If you work hard, we'll have no trouble.'

'Trouble? What kind of trouble?' asked the young man.

'You don't need to know more now. There's never any trouble while the pie man is hungry.'

'Please explain this trouble to me.'

'We'll have time for more conversation later. Good night.' The heavy door closed noisily. Mr Williams heard the key turn in the lock. Then he heard Mrs Lovett's voice again from somewhere above him.

'Remember my orders,' she said. 'And if you try to leave, it will be very dangerous for you.'

'How strange,' thought Mr Williams. 'Why did she say that?' He looked round him. 'This is a really terrible, frightening place! But for now it's beautiful because it's filled with meat pies.'

He sat down and immediately ate twelve of the delicious pies. 'Where does Mrs Lovett get this meat?' he asked himself. 'These pies are wonderful! They're the best, the richest in the world! I've got no friends and no money, and my sweetheart has found somebody new. But now I can eat these wonderful pies until I want to leave. When I'm tired of them, I'll leave England forever. I'll forget about my unkind sweetheart and my forgetful friends. I'll make a new life without them. For now, I'll make pies and eat them as fast as possible.'

The next day Johanna Oakley awoke early and went to her best friend's house.

'Johanna!' cried Arabella Wilmot when she opened the door. 'Where have you been? I haven't seen you for weeks. Come in! You look worried and so serious. Is something wrong?'

Johanna told her friend everything about Mark Ingestrie, Mr Thornhill and his dog, and about her meeting with Mr Jeffery.

'And I had an idea last night,' continued Johanna. 'I know it's strange and probably not possible. But perhaps Mr Thornhill *is* Mark Ingestrie.'

'Dear Johanna,' said Arabella, 'how mysterious! But why is he using a different name?'

'Because he wanted to keep his journey and his fortune secret. He talked about changing his name. I think he *did*. I think he's Mr Thornhill. Mr Jeffery described Thornhill, and his description fits Mark Ingestrie. But where is he now? I must find out.'

'How? What are you going to do?' Arabella asked.

'First, I'm going to meet Mr Jeffery again. I'll ask him some more questions about Mr Thornhill. Then I'll begin to search for him. Either he is Mark Ingestrie or he knows something about him.'

'Johanna, this is so exciting. We'll become detectives and solve this mystery. I've read lots of detective stories. There are many ways to find out about criminals and their activities.'

'But Mark Ingestrie isn't a criminal!'

'Of course not, but something strange has happened to him. And perhaps the barber's a criminal – or even a murderer!'

'Don't say that, Arabella,' cried Johanna. 'Mark Ingestrie has to be alive. I love him with all my heart. Without him I'll be lost, and my life will come to an end.'

Arabella looked at her friend. 'Johanna, this is such a sad story. But we must find your sweetheart. We will, I'm sure! And we'll find your pearl necklace. Perhaps there's something wicked or dangerous about its history. Maybe it brought bad luck to Mark Ingestrie.'

'I've thought of that too. Somebody saw the necklace and wanted it.'

'Oh, yes,' said Arabella. 'It's part of every great romantic story. Everybody wants love and money, but those things bring terrible problems. But the greatest stories end happily. Remember that, Johanna.'

'I will! I'll do anything to find Mark Ingestrie. But what can I do?' cried Johanna.

'Go back to the barber's shop. Surely something happened there. The barber looks like a murderer, doesn't he?'

'Yes, he seems very wicked. But how can I prove anything? I hope that he's a thief and not a murderer!'

'Be calm, dear Johanna. I've got a plan. A short time ago there was a sign in the barber's window. He wanted a boy to work as his assistant. My cousin Albert is your size. With his clothes and hat, you'll look like a young boy. You'll be able to get that job and spy on Mr Sweeney Todd. You can discover his secrets!'

'It will be dangerous, but that doesn't frighten me,' said Johanna.

'And I'll search for you if you don't come home on time,' said Arabella.

'It's an exciting plan,' Johanna said. 'But I'll wait until my next meeting with Mr Jeffery. I want to question him about Thornhill. What does he look like? What kind of man is he? Has Mr Jeffery had any news about him in the last week?'

'Good idea! You're going to be a great detective. But come here immediately after your meeting. Then we'll make plans. We'll solve this mystery!'

Johanna walked home with fresh hope in her heart. Perhaps Mark Ingestrie was in trouble, but was he dead? She didn't think so.

◆

One young person in our story without any hope was poor Tobias Ragg, Sweeney Todd's assistant. To him, the barber was a wicked murderer. But what could he do? He had to protect his mother.

Tobias was beginning to look like an old man with the weight of so many problems on his young shoulders. There were no smiles on his face and there was no happiness in his voice. His world was full of fear and worry, and he could see no way out.

He sat alone in Sweeney Todd's shop with his head in his hands. 'What will happen to me? I'll go crazy if I continue living here. Sweeney Todd is a murderer – I'm quite sure of that. I want to tell the police, but I cannot hurt my mother. And if I do anything, Mr Todd will kill me. Or he'll send me to a home for crazy people.'

The boy's tears fell freely down his face. 'How many men have walked through that door and never left again? How many hats and walking sticks have I found in this shop?'

He looked at the sitting-room door. 'I'd like to find out what's in there. I've been in there with Mr Todd and I've seen lots of cupboards. But they're always locked. There's also an unusual smell in there – something really strange.

'This chair is another unusual thing,' the boy continued to himself. 'Usually a barber's chair can move across the floor, but this one doesn't move. Sweeney Todd says it's better that way. Customers can't move it. And it's in the best light for shaving.'

Sweeney Todd walked silently into the shop. 'Don't you believe me?' he suddenly shouted. 'Don't you remember our last conversation? Don't ever speak about me and my business. One more time and your mother will hang and you will die.'

'I won't forget. I cannot,' Tobias said sadly.

'And why are you so thin? You eat at Mrs Lovett's pie shop every day. Stay silent and stop worrying. Now put a smile on that sad face. There's a customer at the entrance.'

Sweeney Todd looked carefully at the man as he came into the shop.

'Tobias,' the barber said nicely to the boy. 'Go to the market and buy a fish for my supper.'

'Yes,' thought Tobias unhappily. 'Yes, I'll go while you murder your customer.'

◆

Johanna Oakley and Mr Jeffery met for the second time in the Temple Gardens one week later.

'Any news?' Johanna asked immediately.

'I've discovered nothing. But I'm sure that the barber, Sweeney Todd, knows something about Mr Thornhill,' reported Mr Jeffery.

'Sir, does Mr Thornhill have fair hair and large, clear grey eyes? And a beautiful smile?'

'Yes, that's a true description of Thornhill. He's a handsome man – very intelligent and friendly. But why do you ask?'

'I think Thornhill is Mark Ingestrie. You've described him exactly. And he planned to change his name for his journey,' explained Johanna.

'But, Miss Oakley, I don't believe that Mr Thornhill ever left the barber's shop. If he is Mark Ingestrie, he's possibly – even probably – dead.'

'If that's true, I won't live for much longer,' the girl said sadly.

'Don't speak this way. You'll be sad for a long time, but you can find happiness again one day.'

'No, I'll either find Mark Ingestrie or die. I'm not afraid of Sweeney Todd or any other danger. I have nothing to lose.'

'Miss Oakley, you must be careful. Don't do anything dangerous.'

'I'll be sensible, but I won't stop my search.' She decided not to tell Mr Jeffery about Arabella's plan for her.

'I understand,' said Mr Jeffery. 'I'll help you if I can. Shall we meet here again in one week? We'll compare information and possibly succeed. I want to find my good friend, but now, even more, I want to help *you*.'

'Thank you, sir. I'll return in one week if I can.'

◆

Sweeney Todd thought about his problem with the pearl necklace for a number of days. 'How can I sell something so expensive and so beautiful? Who will buy it and wear it? Won't people talk? Won't the police ask questions? "Where did you get that necklace? Who sold it to you? Can you prove that you're the owner?"'

But finally the barber thought of a plan. He left his shop early in the morning. First he bought a suit of fine clothes. Then he went to a barber's shop in a different part of London and paid for a shave and a haircut. Finally he found the best driver, with the finest horses and **carriage** to pick him up at seven o'clock that evening.

Back at home, the barber washed and dressed himself like a prince. When he came out of his sitting-room just before seven o'clock, Tobias was completely surprised. Mr Todd's clothes and boots looked new and very expensive. His rings and walking-stick were also a surprise. The boy was sure that some of these things came from rich customers. And why was the barber wearing a moustache and beard? Was he hiding something? The boy felt that Sweeney Todd had a wicked plan. But what was it? He looked at his boss. But he was too afraid to speak.

'Listen, boy,' said Sweeney Todd, as he left the shop. 'Remember my orders. Then you and your mother will stay alive and happy.'

When he was alone again, Tobias thought, 'Happy? How can we ever be happy again? Why can't I die and be free of this wicked man?'

carriage /ˈkærɪdʒ/ (n) a vehicle with wheels that is pulled by a horse or horses

But we shall leave Tobias with his sad thoughts and follow Mr Todd. Why did he spend a large amount of money on clothes and a carriage? Where was he going? The driver arrived on time and took him outside the city to the house of John Mundel on the Uxbridge Road. Mr Mundel had a very successful business. He lent money to rich people who needed money quickly for a difficult problem or for something special. Later his customers had to return the borrowed money with a lot more for Mr Mundel. He couldn't lose his money because each customer had to leave something valuable with him – jewellery, a painting or a race horse, perhaps – for a week, a month or a year.

At the entrance gates to Mundel House, Sweeney Todd sent his driver to the house to knock on the door. Mr Mundel came out and gave the expensive carriage and fine horses a quick examination. He knew immediately that the man in the carriage was rich and important.

'Welcome to my house, sir,' said John Mundel to the passenger. 'Please come inside. How can I help you?'

'I don't need your help,' said Sweeney Todd. 'I've come on business for an important lady. Please don't ask her name. This is private business, very private!'

Mr Mundel looked at Sweeney Todd's clothes and at his carriage again. Surely this was an important man. He was happy to have him – or the very mysterious lady – as his customer. Was the man a prince? Was the lady the Queen or one of her close relatives?

By the end of the evening Mr John Mundel had the pearl necklace in a safe place in his office. Sweeney Todd had eight thousand pounds in his pocket. He agreed to return the money in one month and take the pearl necklace back to its owner. But, of course, Sweeney Todd didn't plan to return to John Mundel's house – ever.

'That was easy,' Sweeney Todd thought as he travelled in the expensive carriage towards town. 'Now I have plenty of money. I can leave London and start a new life in Belgium. I'll continue my business in Fleet Street for three more months. No sudden changes. I don't want my neighbours to notice anything different about me or my fortune.'

The barber was silent for a few minutes, quietly working on a problem. Then he suddenly said, 'What should I do with Tobias Ragg? It's wiser to kill him. I'm worried about one or two other people too. They must die. Dead men – and women and boys – cannot talk. And finally there will be a big, serious fire on Fleet Street. Sadly, my house and business will disappear. Ha! Ha! The fire will be the sign of the beginning of my new life.'

Sweeney Todd's dark thoughts and dreams continued as he travelled towards the city. He was different from ordinary people. He didn't worry about doing right or wrong. His plans had one purpose only: to make money. Money was the only thing that the barber loved. He enjoyed the journey home, thinking about his clever plans and his growing fortune.

Tobias guessed, and guessed correctly too, the time of Sweeney Todd's return. 'He told me half an hour because he wanted me to wait quietly for him. But in that carriage and in those clothes, he must have an important meeting tonight. He won't be back so soon. But a little more or a little less time isn't important to me. This life is destroying me. Sweeney Todd put his last assistant in the home for crazy people. If I make any trouble for him, he'll put me there too.'

The boy sat down to think. 'Did my mother really steal from her employer? I can't say, "Dear Mother, are you a thief?" She'll hate me if I ask that question. But what will happen if he tells the police about her? My mother will hang because of me! But is his story true? What are the facts?'

Suddenly Tobias jumped to his feet. He had a plan! 'Todd won't return for quite a long time. I'm going to search this house and discover his wicked secrets.'

The boy locked the shop door and then found Sweeney Todd's heavy metal bar. With this tool, Tobias ran towards the sitting-room door. He quickly broke the lock on the door and looked around the room. Most of the cupboards opened easily, but one was locked. Tobias used the metal bar again and soon looked inside. There were hats of every shape and size – more hats than in a hat shop. And as Tobias knew, Sweeney Todd didn't buy hats in hat shops.

Next the boy opened a door in the corner of the room and discovered some stairs. He climbed these to the top of the house and found two empty floors. Then he went down to the first floor and found something quite different. The cupboards were locked, but he used the metal bar on them. He couldn't believe the number of things inside: many very expensive walking-sticks; more than a hundred fine umbrellas; a mountain of very good boots and shoes; piles of gold watches and other jewellery; a large box of cigarette cases, and one complete cupboard full of every type of men's clothes.

'Where did Sweeney Todd get all these wonderful things?' Tobias asked himself. 'That's a silly question! He murdered the owners!'

Tobias looked at everything for another quarter of an hour. 'If my mother and I have a few gold rings, she can stop working.' He started to put three or four rings into his pocket, but he stopped.

'No! These things belong to dead men. They'll carry bad luck with them. Sweeney Todd can enjoy them in his wicked way. I won't touch them.'

Tobias heard St Dunstan's clock – nine o'clock.

'I must go! Sweeney Todd will kill me if he sees his broken locks and open cupboard doors. I want to see my mother's face one last time. But then I'll leave London for a life at sea.' Like many young boys, Tobias had a romantic picture in his mind of life on a ship.

Tobias threw down the heavy metal bar and ran down the stairs. He raced towards the shop's entrance and from there to his mother's poor little house.

◆

Mrs Ragg was very surprised to see her son.

'Mother,' the boy said, 'I cannot stay with Sweeney Todd. Please don't ask me for my reasons.'

'But, son, he's a good man. He's given you a good job,' Mrs Ragg said.

'A good man, Mother! You don't know him very well. But we won't talk about him. That silver box has brought us all this trouble,' cried Tobias.

'But what will you do? And what silver box are you talking about? Are you in trouble?'

'Me! No, of course not, but I have questions about a silver box and Sweeney Todd.'

'No, Tobias, don't say anything on that subject. I don't want to discuss Mr Todd or that box,' said Mrs Ragg.

'Is Mr Todd's story true?'

'Yes, I'm afraid it is. Did he tell you about the box?' asked Mrs Ragg.

'Yes – and now I have the answer to my question. I must go. Goodbye forever, Mother.' Tobias ran out of the place, leaving his mother sad and alone.

'What shall I do?' Mrs Ragg asked herself. 'Mr Todd has surprised me. Why did he tell Tobias about stealing a box? One day he came to my employer's house and shaved him. I saw him put the silver box into his pocket. I went to his shop and discussed things with him sensibly. He listened to me, and I returned the box to my employer's bedroom.

'Since that day, Mr Todd has been a good friend to me. Perhaps he's worried about what I know. But life goes up and down. Tobias seems very worried, perhaps even a little crazy now. But he'll calm down, and maybe then he'll return to his job at the barber's shop. The silver box isn't important to him. He mustn't worry about it.'

◆

Sweeney Todd found a surprise when he returned to his own house. There were no lights burning, and the shop door wasn't locked. Inside he shouted for Tobias, but nobody answered his call. The house was empty.

The barber felt frightened and angry. He searched for matches and soon had light. He walked through the rooms of his house and saw the terrible disorder. He smiled to himself as he thought about Tobias Ragg. He didn't imagine a bright, happy future for the boy. He had a very different idea in his mind for his young assistant.

4.1 Were you right?

Think back to your answers to Activity 3.4. Find examples in Chapter 3 of these, make notes in your notebook.

1 reasons for Mr Skinner's unhappiness

2 Arabella Wilmot's ideas for helping her best friend

3 Johanna Oakley's new idea about Mr Thornhill and Mark Ingestrie

4 Sweeney Todd's lies to Mr John Mundel

5 things that Tobias discovers in Sweeney Todd's cupboards

4.2 What more did you learn?

Make notes about the facts that you have discovered.

1 Name: ....

Description: ....

....

New job: ....

....

2 What: ....

Where: ....

Description: ....

....

Purpose: ....

3 Name: ....

Description: ....

....

Reason: ....

....

4.3 **Language in use**

Look at the sentences on the right. Then match the first parts of the following sentences to the endings, A–H.

> 'If you **can't pay**, you **don't eat** here.'
>
> 'And I**'ll search** for you **if** you **don't come** home on time.'

1 ☐ Mrs Lovett's pie men don't live very long . . .
2 ☐ If she gets a job in the barber's shop, . . .
3 ☐ A customer usually disappears . . .
4 ☐ If they discover any new information, . . .
5 ☐ If Mr Todd leaves the pearl necklace with John Mundel, . . .
6 ☐ Sweeney Todd kills people . . .
7 ☐ If her son goes to sea, . . .
8 ☐ Tobias Ragg won't have a happy future . . .

A if Sweeney Todd finds him.
B if they become a problem for him.
C if they ask questions about her business.
D Johanna and Mr Jeffery will bring it to their next meeting.
E Mrs Ragg will be very sad.
F if Sweeney Todd sends Tobias to the market or to a shop.
G he will return home with eight thousand pounds.
H Johanna will be able to discover Sweeney Todd's secrets.

4.4 **What happens next?**

The first sentence of Chapter 4 is: *It was an exciting time around Fleet Street.* Why is it an exciting time for these people, do you think? Circle a or b.

1 Tobias Ragg
   a He goes to sea on a big ship.
   b He decides to tell the police about Sweeney Todd.

2 Mrs Ragg
   a She feels nervous and very worried about her son.
   b She goes to prison for robbing Mr King.

3 Sweeney Todd
   a He finds Tobias and punishes him.
   b He spends his eight thousand pounds on a new business.

4 Jarvis Williams
   a He falls in love with Mrs Lovett.
   b He begins to question the mysteries in Mrs Lovett's cellar.

CHAPTER 4

Prisoners

If you read these words, you can say goodbye to this world. You will never leave this cellar alive. There is a terrible secret hidden in this place. The secret is . . .

It was an exciting time around Fleet Street. Tobias Ragg was running away to a life at sea. Mr Jarvis Williams was beginning his job as Mrs Lovett's pie man. And Johanna Oakley, Arabella Wilmot, Mr Jeffery and Captain Rathbone were all acting as detectives, hoping to find Mr Thornhill and Mark Ingestrie. During this same unusual season, the people of St Dunstan's began to notice a strange and terrible smell coming from every corner of their church.

'I feel sick when I go into St Dunstan's,' more and more people said.

'I carry a cloth to cover my nose. And that doesn't stop the smell,' said others. 'Or I bring flowers with me and hold them to my nose. But nothing helps!'

'What can we do?' asked the church-workers. 'What's making this terrible smell? Where is it coming from?'

Finally the church officers called a meeting at Mrs Lovett's pie shop, near the entrance to the church in Bell Court.

'We must do something,' said Mr Wilcock, the chief officer. 'People are saying that the smell is a sign of illness and death. We can't have something like this at St Dunstan's. This kind of thing can't happen to people like us.'

'And, Mr Wilcock,' said the church secretary, 'Sir* Robert Mackintosh, the most important church official in this area, is coming next week. It will be a very important visit. We mustn't make Sir Robert ill!'

'We think that the smell started in the cellars under the church,' the workers said. 'But the last dead bodies were put there more than a hundred years ago. They're too old to smell bad.'

The search for the reason for the smell continued but without success.

Sir Robert's carriage arrived on the next Sunday at eleven o'clock in the morning. The great man walked into St Dunstan's, smiled and kindly greeted the crowd of people. After the singing he began his Sunday speech. His speeches were special – full of good teaching and interesting stories – and always very popular. But today the crowd weren't able to enjoy one of Sir Robert's famous talks. He stopped in the middle of a sentence and spoke quietly to Mr Wilcock on his left. 'What's that terrible smell? Is there a dead body in the church?'

Mr Wilcock looked worried. 'No, Sir Robert, it's nothing like that.'

'Is it always here?' asked Sir Robert.

'I'm afraid we've had this problem for many months,' Mr Wilcock reported.

*Sir: a title given to a man by the king or queen for his work

'We're trying to solve it, but without success.'

Sir Robert looked at the crowd and returned to his speech. He finished it quickly and hurried out of the church into the fresh air.

'Mr Wilcock, solve this problem soon! I won't return to St Dunstan's until you do,' he said. Then he climbed into his carriage and left immediately.

Near the church, Sweeney Todd was making a careful examination of his house. 'I can't believe this,' he said to himself. 'That boy has searched every room and opened every cupboard. Was it possible for him to forget my orders?' But as he looked in his cupboards, he saw something surprising. 'That's strange. He's taken nothing. This proves that he's still afraid of me. It won't be difficult to find him.'

The barber took off his beard and moustache and changed into his ordinary clothes. He locked the door and walked towards Mrs Ragg's house, in a poor area of the city. Surely by now she knew where her son was.

Sweeney Todd knocked and Mrs Ragg opened her door very quickly.

'Mrs Ragg, where did your son Tobias go after he left here tonight?'

'Mr Todd, is it you? Tobias *was* here tonight, sir. He says he's going to sea. But he's young and doesn't know his own mind. I don't know where he is.'

'To sea?' Sweeney Todd said. 'Perhaps he's looking for a ship at this minute. But he won't find a job at this time of night. Is he coming back here to sleep?'

'He didn't say,' Mrs Ragg reported. 'But it's possible, isn't it?'

'Did he tell you his reasons for leaving me?'

'No, Mr Todd, he didn't. He seemed different – not the usual Tobias. In fact, he seemed very nervous – a little crazy.'

'I agree with you completely, dear lady. He's acting strangely. I worry about him, as a father worries about a son. We must get help for him before this sickness kills him.'

Sweeney Todd spoke very seriously to Mrs Ragg and she began to agree with him. 'Oh, it's true. He was acting very strangely. And he had secrets that he couldn't tell. That's strange too, isn't it?' asked Mrs Ragg.

'Yes, very strange,' said Mr Todd. 'But listen, Mrs Ragg. What's that noise?'

'It's a knock, Mr Todd. Somebody is at the door. Perhaps it's Tobias.'

'Wait! Before you unlock the door, I'll hide in your cupboard. I'll try to judge the state of his mind. If he's ill, I want to help him. But don't tell him that I'm here. Not yet. Just talk to him. Ask him about his plans.'

The knocking grew louder and Mrs Ragg hurried to the door.

'Mother,' said Tobias, 'I've come back to you. I've had a new idea. I won't go to sea. I'll stay here and tell the police everything. I must!'

'Tobias, what do you mean?' asked Mrs Ragg.

'The silver box isn't important. It's nothing compared to my information,' said the boy.

'But Tobias, the silver box is a secret. You mustn't tell anybody. I put it back and Mr King never knew anything.'

'It's a small matter,' said Tobias. 'Mr King will forgive you. But I must tell somebody my important news.'

'What are you talking about, son? What do you know?'

'I know some terrible things. I cannot tell you alone. Please go to the police station and bring an officer here. Somebody important needs to hear my story. I can save people's lives! Please hurry, Mother!'

'He's crazy,' thought Mrs Ragg. 'Mr Todd's right. Tobias doesn't know what he's talking about. I'll leave the house – then perhaps Mr Todd will talk to him.'

'Son,' Mrs Ragg began loudly, so Todd could hear. 'I'll go to the police. But I hope somebody will speak to you in the next few minutes. Try to stay calm and listen.'

Mrs Ragg left and Tobias sat and waited with his head in his hands.

'Surely my mother won't go to prison,' Tobias said quietly. 'She's innocent compared to a murderer like Sweeney Todd. I know he kills his rich customers.

But how does he do it? And what happens to the bodies?

'The police will solve these mysteries. I've never seen a murder in the shop. I've never found blood anywhere. But when a rich man comes in, I'm always sent out. And if I return too early, I often find a customer's hat or walking stick. Why don't the customers ever come back for these things? The police will search the house and find all those rings and umbrellas and shoes. Then they'll put him in prison. And finally they'll hang him. That'll be a happy day for me!'

But that happy day wasn't part of Tobias Ragg's immediate future. Sweeney Todd's head was full of his own ideas. 'This boy has been a headache to me. I'll finish him before his mother returns. That will solve one of my problems. In fact, I think I'll enjoy this little business. I usually do.' He left his hiding place and silently arrived behind Tobias's chair. He stood there with an ugly, wicked smile on his face, listening to the boy's list of troubles.

'I'll be OK again one day. I'll forget that barber's shop. I'll be at home again with my mother and my life will be happy again. Sweeney Todd is a murderer and I must tell the police. After

that everything will change – everything will be fine. I mustn't be nervous. I must be brave and make things right.'

Tobias suddenly felt Sweeney Todd's large, strong hands around his head. He tried to escape but he couldn't move.

'Tobias Ragg,' growled Sweeney Todd. 'Did you really think that you could run away from me? You'll never escape from me, my boy.'

Tobias was too frightened to speak. But then he screamed very loudly – even Mr Todd was almost frightened. The scream seemed to come from Tobias's heart and reach out towards another world.

The barber dropped his hands for a second. This was dangerous. Were the neighbours listening? But then he put his hands around Tobias's neck. 'If you scream again, it will be your last noise. Now, be quiet or die.'

Of course Tobias couldn't scream because the barber's hands were holding his neck very tightly.

'You're a silly, ungrateful boy,' growled Todd. 'My orders didn't matter to you? How could you imagine winning a war against me? Ha, ha!'

But Tobias didn't hear the barber's wicked laugh. He was no longer able to see or hear. 'So! This is all too much for you, you stupid child. I'll move you now while your mother's looking for a police officer.'

Todd picked up the boy very easily and left the house with him. 'His mother will understand that he's with me,' he thought. 'She won't worry about him – but I can't kill him. She'll remember that I was here tonight.'

The barber walked quickly back to Fleet Street carrying the young boy. At the market he found a number of carriages waiting for business. 'Take us to Peckham Rye. Be quick!' he told one of the drivers. Then he placed Tobias on the floor of the vehicle and rested his very large feet on the boy's back.

As they travelled through the night, Sweeney Todd spoke to the boy, though Tobias could hear nothing. 'Well, boy, your troubles will soon be at an end. You'll have a new home after tonight, but not for long. I'm really afraid that you'll die suddenly. Nobody will know the reasons for your death. Nobody will even notice. No one will feel sad. You'll simply disappear from this world.'

Finally the carriage arrived at a big, lonely old house in the middle of nowhere. Sweeney Todd knocked at the gate and waited. A tall, rough-looking man unlocked the heavy door and let the man and boy inside.

'Ah, it's Mr Todd again,' said the man. 'Have you got a new patient for us? Is he quiet or will I need some help with him?'

'There won't be any problems with him, Mr Watson. He's just a boy and he's asleep. But he's crazy. Don't believe anything he says to you,' Sweeney Todd explained.

'He can say what he likes. We don't believe anything they say. This is a home for crazy people. You know that. I'll put him in a safe place. Go to the office and talk to Mr Fogg. You know where to find him.'

◆

Sweeney Todd knocked on the door of Mr Fogg's office. A voice cried, 'Who knocks? Who knocks? Why is someone at my door at this hour?'

The barber didn't answer, but walked into the room. Inside he found Mr Fogg, an old man with a long grey beard. He was sitting at a desk which was covered with books and papers and glasses and bottles. On the walls were all sorts of tools. These were used to keep the patients in order – or were they prisoners? The name didn't matter. The unhappy people in this terrible place could never leave.

'Mr Todd, my good friend,' said Mr Fogg as the barber walked into his office. 'You're not an easy man to forget.' The owner of the place reached for a large book on the shelf behind him. It said *Fogg's Special Hospital* on the cover. He opened the book to the letter T. 'Mr Sweeney Todd, Fleet Street, London, paid for one year's bed and food for Thomas Simkins, aged thirteen. Then, a short time later, paid the full cost of putting the same boy into the ground after his death. He was found dead in his bed if I remember correctly. Now, what can I do for you today, sir?'

'I'm not very lucky with my boys,' reported Todd. 'I've got another boy here who has lost his mind. It's become necessary to place him in your special hospital. He says that I, the kindest employer in the world, am a murderer.'

'A murderer! You, Mr Todd! That is a crazy thing to say. How long do you think this illness will last?' asked Fogg.

'I'll pay for twelve months. But I think he'll die suddenly before that. What do you think?' Todd asked.

'It's possible, very possible. Many of our patients do die suddenly. We often find them dead in their beds in the morning. We take the bodies out quickly and quietly. We don't like to make life more difficult, or more expensive, for the dead patient's family or friends,' explained Fogg.

'Very correct in every way,' the barber agreed.

'You know my rules, Mr Todd. I try to help when I can. I don't ask questions and I keep my opinions to myself. That's why I have a successful business. And that's why customers return to me. Now, where's my new patient?'

The two men found Tobias in an examination room with Mr Watson.

'He's quite young,' said Mr Fogg, looking at the pale, interesting face of Tobias.

'Look, he's opening his eyes. Perhaps he'll speak.'

'It won't mean anything. He doesn't know what he's talking about,' said Sweeney Todd. 'He's lost his mind, but listen to him.'

'Where am I?' said Tobias in a weak voice. He looked at Mr Fogg and said, 'Todd is a murderer. Tell the police.'

'I can see that he's crazy,' said the wicked Fogg.

'No, please protect me, sir. Men come into his shop and never leave again. He's a murderer. Please believe me,' cried Tobias. 'He wants to kill me. Search his house on Fleet Street near St Dunstan's church. You'll find hundreds of hats and boxes of jewellery and clothes and umbrellas and walking-sticks. They belong to his dead customers. I don't know how he kills them. But I know that he does!'

'What an unusual story!' said Fogg. 'I've heard enough. Mr Watson, shave his head and put him in a dark room in the cellar. Too much light will make him worse. Remember to lock the door. I think he's dangerous.'

'No! No! Please listen to me,' cried Tobias. 'What crime have I done? Why am I here? Please, someone, believe me. I'm not crazy!'

'Watson, give him only bread and water. We'll try to make him healthy again. But he mustn't talk about his employer in this way. Mr Todd is a good, honest man,' Fogg said.

'No, you can't say that. Sweeney Todd is a murderer. If he's good and honest, then I really am crazy,' cried Tobias.

'Take him away, Watson,' said Mr Fogg. 'He's crazier than most of our patients. And I believe he's dangerous.'

Mr Watson was a very large, very strong man. He picked Tobias Ragg up with one hand and began to carry him out of the room. Tobias screamed. But before the boy went through the door, Sweeney Todd stepped out of the shadows. He put his mouth close to the boy's ear and said quietly, 'How do you

feel now, boy? Do you think I'll hang? Or do you think you'll die in a cold, dark room in this place?'

With Tobias out of the room, Sweeney Todd threw his head back and laughed. He made a terrible noise which surprised even Mr Fogg.

'Mr Todd, I see that you still have your laugh. It's not the most pleasant sound in the world, is it? It's worse than anything I hear from my patients.'

'Mr Fogg, you're forgetting that I'm your customer. I think I'd like a glass of something before my journey back to Fleet Street.'

'Mr Todd, can I offer you a glass of one of the best wines in the country? I've heard that it's the king's favourite drink. You see, sometimes the families of my patients begin to feel sorry for their relatives in here. They send them some very nice gifts. This wine, for example, was sent by a very rich family to their grandfather, but he's better with water. And I feel better – and calmer – with this fine wine on my table.'

'While I'm enjoying your wine, I'll also pay you. I remember your rule about immediate payment. I'd like to pay for one year.' Todd handed the correct amount of money to Mr Fogg.

'Mr Todd, I'm pleased to do business with my favourite customer,' Mr Fogg said. 'Please have another glass of this excellent wine. Your problem is solved and we can now enjoy ourselves as two very successful businessmen.'

◆

And what happened to Tobias Ragg? He was carried down many stairs to a cold, dark cellar. Finally he was thrown into a terrible room: dirty, empty and cold with no light or furniture.

'I'm not crazy!' he cried to Mr Watson. 'Show me the way out and I'll say nothing. Not one word about Mr Todd will ever come out of my mouth!'

Mr Watson smiled and sang a happy little song to himself. He pushed Tobias into the corner of the room and gave him a hard kick.

'Sir, I won't hurt Mr Todd,' cried Tobias. 'Please, be kind to me.'

'*Kind?* What do you mean by that? *Be kind?* That's a good joke in a place like this. You'll have to go to a different sort of hospital to find a kind person. Ha, ha!' Then he left Tobias alone. He walked up the stairs again, singing.

Tobias lay on his back, feeling afraid and lonely. 'I'll never see the blue sky and green fields again. I'm going to die here because I know Mr Todd's secrets. Why did I return to my mother's house? Oh, what was that? Another terrible scream. This place is full of crazy people. Or perhaps they aren't crazy – maybe they're like me and they're here for no good reason.

'Help! Help!' Tobias screamed. 'I'll do anything. I want to go home.' But, of course, nobody was listening.

Tobias listened to the other screams as he looked at the dark walls around him. He began to see ugly, frightening faces of strange, unreal people and animals. Did they come from his mind or did they live in this terrible world? He covered his eyes but the faces didn't disappear. With this company around him, Tobias knew that he couldn't last long in this terrible place.

◆

Back in the centre of London, near Fleet Street, another young man was beginning to feel like a prisoner. It was Jarvis Williams's fourth day in Mrs Lovett's cellar and finally he had a full stomach. The job wasn't difficult and he could eat delicious pies all day long. He tried them hot and cold, with salt and without salt, cooked and half-cooked. But on this day he noticed that he didn't want another pie.

'I know how the pies are made,' Mr Williams said. 'There's nothing wrong with them. But who knows where the meat comes from? It simply arrives on the shelves every day.'

That morning Mr Williams looked at a pie for a few minutes and then threw it on the table. 'I can't live only on pies,' he cried. 'I can't eat another one.'

Suddenly he heard a noise above him. He looked up. The window near the roof opened. 'Hello! Hello! Mrs Lovett? Is that you?'

A bag dropped to the floor and the window was shut.

'This is terrible!' shouted Mr Williams. 'I'm like these machines. I'm a prisoner in this dark cellar.' The young man began to look carefully around him. 'I'm not hungry now and can think more clearly. Is there a way to escape from this cellar? The meat arrives on the stone shelves in some way. But how? Through hidden doors? Does somebody put things on the shelves when I'm asleep? This is very mysterious. Meat can't arrive from nowhere. But fresh meat is always here when I need it.'

There was one heavy door, but he couldn't find any other doors or windows. But he did find something unusual. On a stone at the bottom of one wall he

noticed some writing. It was difficult to read. But finally Mr Williams understood the words.

If you read these words, you can say goodbye to this world. You will never leave this cellar alive. There is a terrible secret hidden in this place. The secret is . . .

The writing ended there. Jarvis Williams felt angry and afraid. He looked more carefully at the stones along the floor but didn't find any more writing.

'This is worse than no information. What's going to happen to me? What secrets are hidden in this cellar?'

Then, as he walked towards the shelf with the meat, the young pie man stepped on a clean piece of paper. How did a new, white piece of paper arrive on the cellar floor? He picked it up with a shaking hand. What did it say? Was it something terrible? He read this short note:

You're not hungry but you're feeling unhappy. It's time to understand your real position. You're a prisoner. You'll be safe if you continue to make the pies. If you don't make the pies, you'll die. You'll go to sleep and never wake up.

'No!' shouted Jarvis Williams. 'This isn't possible! Is this a dream? Surely I cannot be a prisoner in the centre of London. How can Mrs Lovett do this? It's too terrible to be true.'

He sat on the old, hard chair where Mr Skinner died. 'Are there enemies on every side of me? Will I be murdered as I sit here in the dark? I'm a brave man, but I can't fight against the mysteries around me.'

He jumped up and ran to the big door. He hit it, kicked it, shook it. But the door was too strong and heavy. He fell into the chair again, feeling weak and helpless.

Then he heard a voice and he saw a face in the small window far above him. But this time it wasn't the face of Mrs Lovett. It was a large, ugly male face.

'Continue your work,' growled the deep voice. 'If you don't, you'll die tonight. Continue your work and you'll escape death.'

'Why are you doing this to me? I don't know your secrets. I can't hurt you,' shouted Williams.

'Make pies,' said the voice, 'eat them and be happy. You've got everything you need: a home, food, work. Be grateful.' Then the window was shut loudly.

'Am I going crazy?' Jarvis Williams said to himself. 'Can this be happening to me? I feel so tired. But if I close my eyes, I'll die.' He felt sorry for himself for a few minutes, but then he jumped up again. 'I'm not ready to die. I still have some hope and I must find a way out of here.'

He hurried to the ovens and prepared them for the next tray of pies. Soon these were cooked and on the lift to the shop. The pie man was able to sleep again without worries, for another night.

5.1 Were you right?

Look back at your answers to Activity 4.4. Then write the places that these people go to in Chapter 4. Finally, discuss why they are in each place.

1 Tobias Ragg:

In Mrs Ragg's house → In a .... → In a dark room at ....
....

2 Mrs Ragg:

In her house → At the .... station

3 Mr Todd:

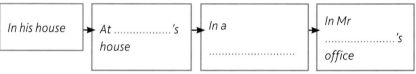

In his house → At ....'s house → In a .... → In Mr ....'s office

4 Mr Williams:

In Mrs ....'s cellar

5.2 What more did you learn?

What do these tell us about the story? Find an answer on the right, and draw a line to it.

1 The smell in St Dunstan's Church

2 Mrs Ragg speaking loudly

3 Thomas Simkins

4 Mr Watson's singing, Sweeney Todd's laugh, Mr Fogg's tools

5 Frightening pictures in Tobias's head

6 The note on Mrs Lovett's cellar floor

a People soon go crazy in Mr Fogg's hospital.

b There is something unusual under the floor.

c Pie men don't leave their job at Mrs Lovett's alive.

d The home for crazy people is a dangerous, wicked place.

e Sweeney Todd murders more than customers and pie men.

f Sweeney Todd will have some time alone with Tobias.

3.3 Language in use

Look at the sentences on the right.
Then complete these sentences in
the same way.

> 'They're **too old to smell** bad.'
>
> Tobias was **too frightened to speak**.

1 Sir Robert Mackintosh feels ....*too sick to stay*...... very long in St Dunstan's.
   (sick, stay)

2 Tobias is .... of bad luck .... from
   Sweeney Todd. (afraid, steal)

3 Tobias's news is .... only his mother.
   (important, tell)

4 Mrs Ragg is .... clearly. (worried, think)

5 Mr Fogg's wine is .... to his patients.
   (good, give)

6 Jarvis Williams is .... the short note on
   the cellar floor. (surprised, believe)

3.4 What happens next?

Look at the five pictures in Chapter 5. Discuss what is happening. What do you
think is going to happen next? Write a sentence.

1 ....
   ....

2 ....
   ....

3 ....
   ....

4 ....
   ....

5 ....
   ....

CHAPTER 5

Help Is Found

'I'll kill that boy,' Mr Fogg thought angrily.
'He can't do something like that in my hospital.'

Mr Jeffery couldn't rest while Mr Thornhill was still missing. Working night and day, with the help of Captain Rathbone, he continued his search for his friend. The two men made a careful examination of the facts and were sure of two things. Number one: Sweeney Todd wasn't an innocent man, but what exactly were his crimes? Number two: the barber's boy knew something about Todd's crimes. But he was afraid to say anything.

'Mr Todd has frightened the boy almost to death,' said Captain Rathbone. 'Fear keeps him silent. We can use fear too. If we frighten him, he'll talk to us. Then we can protect him from the barber.'

The two men went to a pub on Fleet Street early in the morning and sat at a table next to a window. From there they could watch the barber's shop. They hoped to catch Tobias Ragg when he was alone in the shop.

It was a good plan but there was, of course, one problem. Tobias wasn't in London. The poor boy was already locked up in Fogg's Special Hospital. So Mr Sweeney Todd's secrets were also locked up.

As they waited, the two men talked about many subjects.

'We mustn't forget Miss Oakley's problems,' said Captain Rathbone. 'Is there any news about her missing sweetheart? What's his name?'

'Mark Ingestrie,' answered Mr Jeffery. 'She believes that he and Thornhill may be the same person.'

'Is that possible?' asked Rathbone.

'I don't think so. But I have a very high opinion of Miss Oakley and want to help her if possible. I hope we'll soon discover something about both Ingestrie and Thornhill.'

'Soon? Look! It's the barber. He's just arrived at his shop. Has he travelled all night?'

In fact Mr Todd was returning from his night as the guest of Mr Fogg. He looked tired and dirty because of Mr Fogg's wine and because of his long journey home in bad weather on foot.

The two detectives watched as the barber looked in every pocket for his key. They couldn't hear his words, but Sweeney Todd was talking to himself during his search.

'No more trouble from Tobias Ragg!' he said. 'Mr Fogg is a very useful friend. Some of these boys ask too many questions. For very little money, Fogg solves

50

that sort of problem. Tobias Ragg's questions and searches have stopped forever.

'Now I'd like to leave this business and this city. With the eight thousand pounds from the pearl necklace, and the rest of my fortune, I can start a new life. After a month John Mundel can sell the necklace. But I mustn't hurry. There are people who are looking for it and its owner. I don't want them to ask any more questions about me and the pearls. I must keep quiet until this business is finished.'

Finally he opened his door and disappeared inside.

'This is interesting,' said Mr Jeffery. 'He's been out of town, hasn't he?'

'I'm sure you're right. Did you notice his clothes and his dirty boots? Look, he's coming outside again. He's opening the windows and sweeping the entrance. Why isn't the boy doing those jobs?' said Captain Rathbone.

'Where *is* the boy?' asked Jeffery. 'Are Todd's activities of last night tied to the boy's disappearance in some way?'

'I'm afraid they are. But there may be another reason for Tobias's disappearance.'

'Yes, but I think Todd's a murderer. Perhaps he murdered the boy during the night. Look at the shop! The barber has his first customer of the day.'

The detectives saw a handsome, expensively dressed businessman stop in front of the barber's shop. He was carrying a small suitcase, so he was a visitor to London. After a minute or two the man decided to go into the shop for a shave.

Jeffery and Rathbone saw the door close behind the man. They weren't interested in him. They were thinking about Tobias Ragg and watching for his return. But after a number of minutes they saw another customer go into the barber's shop. This second man came out after about five minutes with a clean face.

Mr Jeffery looked at Captain Rathbone. 'Am I right or wrong?' he asked. 'Has the first customer – the one with the suitcase – come out of the barber's shop?'

'No, he hasn't. We haven't left this window. We know he's still inside!'

'The barber has killed him! I'm sure of this. I think he killed Thornhill in the same way. I'm going across the street. He's a murderer!' cried Jeffery.

'Wait! You don't know how dangerous Todd is. You can't go in there alone. I won't let you. We need a plan – and we need some help. You've heard, of course, of Sir Richard Blunt?'

'Blunt? You mean the High Court judge?'

'I do. He's a great friend of mine. We'll go to him and explain everything. His opinions are always valuable. But we must act quickly. There have been enough murders in that barber's shop.'

◆

At Sir Richard Blunt's office, the judge listened carefully as Mr Jeffery told him about Sweeney Todd and about the disappearance of Mr Thornhill, Tobias Ragg and the customer with the suitcase. 'It's very mysterious. We aren't sure how to continue. How can we prove that the barber is a murderer?'

'First,' began Sir Richard, 'I'll go to Fleet Street for a shave. Don't worry, I won't be in any danger. I'll take someone to protect me. I've heard about Mr Todd before.

'About a year ago a lady went to a theatre in the city. She screamed when she saw her missing husband's ring on a man's finger. The husband was never seen again after he went out for a shave one morning. You can probably guess who was wearing the ring. But sadly the ring was a very popular type. The woman couldn't prove that it was her husband's. So I couldn't put Todd in prison.'

'But you haven't forgotten about him,' said Captain Rathbone.

'No, I haven't. I'd like to prove that he's a criminal. Sweeney Todd belongs in prison,' the judge said.

'Thank you very much. You're a good friend,' added Captain Rathbone.

'And how are my old friends at St Dunstan's Church?' Sir Richard asked. 'Do you go there every Sunday?'

'Hasn't anybody told you about St Dunstan's? Nobody goes in there now. There's a terrible smell in the church. It makes people ill.'

'Really?' Sir Richard said. 'The church is very near to Sweeney Todd's shop, isn't it?'

◆

That afternoon Sir Richard Blunt went to St Dunstan's Church alone. He found Mr Wilcock and asked him about the smell.

'Where's it coming from? What are you doing about it?' the judge asked.

'Sir, it's a mystery. We're moving the stones from the floor and looking under it today,' explained Mr Wilcock.

'Can I stay and watch your work?' Sir Richard asked. 'I have some ideas about this problem, and they're quite frightening.'

'Of course. You're very welcome here. Perhaps you'll be able to solve this mystery for us,' Mr Wilcock said. He and Sir Richard watched as the workmen lifted a number of very large stones.

'Mr Wilcock, St Dunstan's troubles are greater than you can imagine. Look into the space below the stones. Can you see those stairs? You and I will go down there. Send the workmen away immediately. I think we're getting very close to solving this mystery.'

The two men walked slowly down the steps into a cold, dark room. At the end there was a door. When they opened it, the smell became even stronger. Sir Richard went through the door while Mr Wilcock waited. He returned very quickly.

'I've seen enough. I know what the secret is,' said Sir Richard. 'We can return to the church and I'll make my report to you and then to the police. Mr Wilcock, please lock the outside door of the church and keep everybody out.'

◆

What was Tobias Ragg thinking as he lay on the floor of his dark room in Fogg's Special Hospital? The boy knew that he wasn't crazy. But he believed that his mind couldn't stay healthy for very long in such a place. He went in and out of a dream world, imagining strange animals and bloody knives in the darkness around him. He was too afraid to make a sound.

Mr Fogg and Mr Watson were happy to forget about quiet patients. Hours could pass and poor people like Tobias didn't hear another person.

But Tobias awoke from his bad dreams when he heard the sound of singing very near to him. It was a female voice – sweet and musical – and Tobias felt a little better. 'Oh, I hope that singing doesn't stop. What sweet music!

'Who can she be?' Tobias asked himself. 'She's sung the same song many times. Is she crazy? Will she be here until she dies?' This idea frightened Tobias and he shouted, 'Help! Help!' in a very loud voice.

The singing stopped and the female voice screamed. The sound filled the boy with fear, and very soon Mr Watson arrived outside the singer's room.

'Do you want my stick so early in the morning?' Watson asked in a rough voice. Then the stick came down on the girl, but she didn't scream. She cried very softly. This sound touched poor Tobias's heart.

'I can't live here. I'll go crazy.' And then he shouted again: 'Help! Help!' He needed to talk to somebody, to hear a kind voice.

Finally Mr Watson came back and unlocked the door to Tobias's room.

'Please help me!' Tobias cried.

But there was no kindness from Mr Watson. Tobias felt the stick across his back. 'Is that what you wanted, boy? Do you know what *I* want? I want silence and I'll get it with my stick. Do you understand?'

'Yes, sir, I understand. But please understand *me*. I'm innocent and not crazy. I want to go home. I'll say nothing about Mr Todd and his secrets. I promise.'

Mr Watson closed the door and locked it. He sang a happy little song as he walked away from Tobias and the other patients.

◆

Tobias had no idea of the time of day, but finally Mr Watson and Mr Fogg returned. They went into each room and Tobias could hear screams and shouts. He could also hear the sound of Mr Watson's stick as he hit the patients.

'We're kept like wild animals,' Tobias thought. 'They don't talk to us or listen to us. They hit us but they don't worry about our health or the state of our minds.'

Finally the boy's door was opened and the two men came inside. Mr Watson poured a cup of dirty water into Tobias's mouth. Mr Fogg threw an old loaf of bread onto the floor.

'Wait!' shouted Tobias as the two men turned to leave. 'Please! I'll say nothing about Todd. I'll go to sea immediately. I won't make any trouble for you or for Mr Todd. If you leave me here, I'll go crazy.'

'He's a clever boy, isn't he, Watson?' said Mr Fogg.

'Very clever, sir. He's one of the cleverest people in this place. You can't imagine what they say to me sometimes,' answered Watson.

'But really, I'm not crazy!' cried Tobias.

'Oh, he's in a bad state, I'm afraid,' replied Mr Fogg. 'The craziest ones repeat the same words again and again. We won't tie him up today because we're going to have a visit from good Dr Popplejoy. He's always happy to earn ten pounds for nothing. He's eighty-four years old now and can't see much. He'll do his usual examination of the hospital. Then I'll write a report and he'll sign it.

'Popplejoy gets his money and I can show my customers the report. It proves that this is a clean, healthy place for patients. The old doctor will be here at twelve o'clock, so clean that boy.'

Tobias listened carefully to the two men. He planned to speak to this doctor and tell him his story.

◆

At twelve o'clock the old doctor arrived at Fogg's Special Hospital, as he did once a year, to check the place and the patients.

'Good afternoon, Dr Popplejoy,' Mr Fogg began. 'It's nice to see you. You're always so kind to me and to my patients. We always look forward to your report because we want to look after these patients in the kindest, the best possible way. Watson, please show the doctor one of the patient's bedrooms.'

Watson took the doctor into a very pleasant, comfortable, bright room.

'Very good,' the old doctor said. 'And what sort of food do the patients eat?'

'Everything is very fresh. We worry about their health. They also get a lot of fresh air and exercise,' reported Fogg.

'Also very good. Now, can I see the patients?' the old man requested.

The old doctor sat in a comfortable chair in Mr Fogg's office with a nice glass of wine in his hand. Watson brought in the patients – all clean and very quiet – one at a time. The doctor smiled at them but he didn't look at them closely. He was quite happy in his nice chair with his glass of excellent wine.

Tobias Ragg was the last patient for Dr Popplejoy to see.

'This is a very young boy, Mr Fogg!' the doctor said in surprise. 'Why is he here?'

'Doctor, it's very sad. My heart breaks every time I look at him. He has a crazy idea about a man named Sweeney Todd. He thinks the man's a murderer.'

'Who is this man?' asked the doctor.

'Sir, that's the problem. This Sweeney Todd doesn't exist. The boy has imagined him and his crimes.'

'No, doctor, please, don't listen to him. I'm *not* crazy. Sweeney Todd kills the customers in his barber's shop,' cried Tobias. 'Sir, wicked Mr Todd brought me here because I discovered his crimes.'

'Sad,' said the doctor. 'Very sad. Be calm, little boy. Mr Fogg will help you, I'm sure.'

'Please, sir, don't believe him,' cried Tobias. 'This is a terrible place, and Mr Fogg is a wicked man. Please believe me. I'm not crazy.'

'I'm sorry, doctor. He's very ill. Watson, take him back to his room,' ordered Mr Fogg. 'Tell him a nice bedtime story and give him a cup of hot milk.'

'Yes,' said the doctor. 'That's what he needs.'

◆

Outside Tobias's room, Mr Watson gave the boy a hard kick. 'That didn't help you, did it?' he said.

This was too much for the angry, frightened boy. He attacked Watson like a wild animal. He hit the man in his face and eyes and pulled his hair. Watson was a big man but he wasn't prepared for this attack. He fell and hit his head on the stone floor. Tobias continued hitting him until Mr Fogg arrived. He pulled the boy away from Mr Watson and threw him into his room.

'I'll kill that boy,' Mr Fogg thought angrily. 'He can't do something like that in my hospital.' But he had to wait because old Dr Popplejoy was still sitting in his office.

◆

Tobias was alone again in his room and his mind was full of dark ideas. 'They'll murder me now. My life has ended. But why are they waiting? I'd like to be dead and out of this ugly place, away from these terrible people.'

He hurried from one side of his room to the other, unable to rest or stay quiet. He ran to the door and hit it with his shoulder. To his surprise, the door opened. Suddenly Tobias was outside his dark room.

'How did *that* happen?' Tobias asked himself. 'Perhaps I hurt Mr Watson quite badly and he forgot about my door. But now what can I do to get out of this place? Maybe I *will* see the blue sky again and my mother's face if I think carefully. I must – I *will* be free!'

His heart was racing and he had to calm himself. Finally he looked around and saw the doors to other rooms. He walked past these doors silently, listening carefully. Then suddenly he heard the sound of people walking towards him. He was very frightened, but the people turned and disappeared behind a door. Tobias hurried there and put his ear against the door. He could hear a conversation between his enemies: Mr Fogg and Mr Watson.

'You understand my orders, Watson, I think,' Mr Fogg said. 'Todd's boy is too clever. He's too dangerous to keep here. Popplejoy almost believed his story.'

'And look what he did to me!' shouted Watson.

'I think he'll die in his bed tonight. What's your opinion on that, Watson?'

'I think so too,' said Watson. 'But I won't go near him until tonight. Without food or water he'll calm down. Then there won't be any trouble from him later.'

'We've agreed on that,' Mr Fogg said. 'Now it's time for you to check the other patients.'

Hearing this, Tobias ran back to the patients' rooms. He pushed the door next to his. Surprisingly that door also opened. Tobias saw a young woman lying on the floor.

'No, please, not the stick. I'll be quiet,' she cried. She thought that Mr Watson was at her door.

'Be quiet, please!' said Tobias very kindly. 'I'm a friend. I've escaped from the room next to yours. Can you hide me? Watson's coming!'

'Another prisoner? You're a young boy. What are you doing in a place like this?'

'There's no time for talking. Please save me! He's getting closer.'

'Don't be afraid. You're safe with me,' the young woman said. 'I'll cover you with my old clothes in the corner. Mr Watson doesn't come in here. He looks through the door and throws some bread at me. If I'm quiet, he goes away. If you stay here until night, I'll show you the way out of here.'

Mr Watson came to the woman's room. 'You've got enough bread and water until tomorrow. You won't see me again tonight,' he growled, and locked the door.

'We're saved!' the woman said to Tobias. 'We can escape tonight.'

'Really? Do you really think so?' asked Tobias. 'They want to murder me tonight. I heard them making their plans.'

'Listen. I've been here for many years. The floor is made of large stones, but I can move one of them. Each day I've worked on my escape. I've made a **tunnel** from this room to the wall outside, across the garden, but I can't climb over the wall without help. You're young and strong. If we both go through the tunnel late tonight, you can climb over the wall. Then you can help me, and we'll be free.'

'No wall can stop me!' Tobias said excitedly.

The two new friends had a long evening in front of them. During that time they told the stories of their journey to Fogg's Special Hospital. First the woman heard about Sweeney Todd, and then she told Tobias about her wicked family.

'When I was a young girl, my favourite aunt died. She left me a large fortune, but it wasn't mine until my eighteenth birthday. From the day of her death my life was terrible. The idea of this fortune changed my parents. They began to hate me because they wanted my aunt's money. But then, when I was almost eighteen, I met a young man. We fell in love. We wanted to marry, but my parents didn't like that plan. One night they put me in a carriage and brought me here. They told Mr Fogg that I was crazy. He agreed to keep me. Of course they paid him a lot of money, and I've been a prisoner since then. My parents are at home enjoying my fortune.'

tunnel /ˈtʌnl/ (n) a long hole made under the ground or through a mountain

From the sound of the church clock, Tobias and the young woman knew that it was ten o'clock. It was time for their escape. They both went through the tunnel quite easily. Tobias climbed the tree next to the wall and in three minutes he was on top of the wall. The moon shone brightly and the boy felt the clean, fresh air on his face.

'Tobias! Quickly! Help me to climb the wall,' cried the young woman. Tobias held one end of his jacket and dropped the other end to the woman. 'Hold on to the jacket. Can you climb up? Don't hurry. We've got all night.'

'Yes, yes!' said the woman as she began to climb. 'I'm coming! I'm saved!'

Tobias held the jacket and spoke kindly to her. 'Come slowly.' But the thin jacket was pulled into two pieces. The young woman fell to the ground.

Lights came on in the house. People were shouting. They knew that a patient was missing. What could Tobias do? Two people couldn't be saved, but one could. He turned and jumped down on the other side of the wall. He was hurt from the drop, but nothing mattered. He was free! He hurried towards London with one idea in his head. 'Sweeney Todd will go to prison. I'll make sure of that,' he thought.

6.1 Were you right?

Put these in the right order. Write the numbers 1–8.

A ☐ A female patient hides Tobias when Watson is checking the rooms.

B ☐ Tobias discovers that the door to his room isn't locked.

C ☐ Tobias escapes from his prison but leaves his friend behind.

D ☐ Old Dr Popplejoy visits Mr Fogg's Special Hospital.

E ☐1 Jeffery and Rathbone notice that Tobias isn't at work.

F ☐ Tobias attacks Mr Watson.

G ☐ Sir Richard Blunt discovers the reason for the bad smell in St Dunstan's Church.

H ☐ A rich man with a suitcase goes into the barber's shop and doesn't come out again.

6.2 What more did you learn?

Discuss these people's opinions of Sweeney Todd, and the reasons for their opinions.

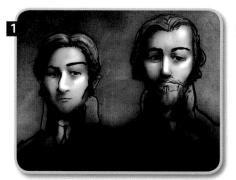

6.3 Language in use

Look at the sentences on the right.
Then complete the sentences below.

'He's a clever boy, **isn't he**, Watson?'

'That didn't help you, **did it**?'

1 Sweeney Todd has murdered the businessman with the suitcase,

....?

2 Sir Richard Blunt already knows a lot about Sweeney Todd, ...?

3 The bad smell in the church is a mystery, ...?

4 Mr Wilcock and the church workers can't solve the problem, ...?

5 Tobias and his new friend don't belong in a crazy house, ...?

6 Dr Popplejoy isn't able to help the patients, ...?

7 Watson, Fogg and Todd are wicked men, ...?

8 Tobias's new friend probably won't ever escape from Mr Fogg's

Special Hospital, ...?

6.4 What happens next?

1 Answer the questions. Who do you think . . .

    a gets a job in Sweeney Todd's shop? ....

    b poisons Mrs Lovett? ....

    c discovers the terrible secret about the meat in Mrs Lovett's ....
       delicious pies?

    d proves that Sweeney Todd is a murderer? ....

    e is hanged? ....

2 Work with another student. Have this conversation.

| Student A | You are Sweeney Todd. You are talking to a boy who wants to work in your shop. Is he the right kind of boy for you? Ask him questions. |

| Student B | You really need a job, and you want to work for Sweeney Todd. Answer his questions, and ask questions about the work. |

CHAPTER 6

The Last Tray of Pies

'Dear customers, I'm afraid I'm going to destroy your happy evening. But it's always good to have the facts.'

There was a sign in Sweeney Todd's window: *Wanted: a boy. Job: to help the barber. Must be clean, tidy and serious. Must follow orders. Knock on the door.*
'Yes!' Johanna Oakley said to herself. 'Here's the way to discover more about the barber. It's probably dangerous, but my life means nothing without Mark Ingestrie.'

'Who's this?' Sweeney Todd asked himself. 'A pretty-looking boy is reading my sign. Does he really *need* a job?'

The barber opened the door and asked, 'Who are you? Why do *you* want a job?'

Johanna, dressed as a boy, had her story ready. 'My parents are dead, sir. I have to live with my wicked aunt. I ran away and now I must find a job.'

'Where did you come from?'

'From Oxford. I don't know anybody here.'

'But your aunt will look for you,' said the barber.

'No, sir, she hates me. She'll be happy that I'm gone.'

'Well, I'll give you the job because you're alone in the world. No friends or family who will worry about you. What's your name, boy?'

'Charley Green, sir. I'll work hard for you, I promise,' Johanna said.

'You can begin now. I'm going out. Stay here and watch the shop. Sit and don't touch anything. If you don't follow my orders, you'll be very sorry.'

Sweeney Todd walked quickly down Pickett Street to the chemist's.

'Good morning, Mr Todd,' said the chemist's assistant. 'How can I help you today?'

'I need some more poison. It's important to keep my shop clean. There are animals under the floor. I use it on them,' explained the barber.

'Use one or two drops of this poison mixed with water. Put it in the corners of the room. But be careful with it. Ten or twelve drops of it can kill a man.'

'Thank you. It's going to rain today, isn't it?' said Todd calmly.

Then the barber walked away with the poison in his pocket. 'This will help me with my plan for leaving London. But I must stay quiet about that. If Mrs Lovett finds out, she'll want half of my money.'

◆

'At last I'm alone in this mysterious place,' said Johanna Oakley. 'Did Mark Ingestrie come in here for a shave and never leave? Or has he disappeared for another reason? I must look around while Mr Todd is out.' She looked into the cupboard and saw a number of expensive walking sticks and some umbrellas. She made a careful examination of the barber's chair. She noticed that she couldn't move it.

'Can I break the lock on the sitting-room door?' she asked herself.

At that minute somebody opened the door. 'I saw Mr Todd go out,' the stranger said. 'Please read this letter but hide it from the barber. It's from Sir Richard Blunt, the judge.' He gave the letter to Johanna and left.

The girl's fingers were shaking as she read the note:

Miss Oakley, your friend Arabella Wilmot became frightened for you and went to Mr Jeffery. He told me about you. Do not be afraid. My officers and I will protect you from Mr Todd. Be prepared. When the sun goes down this evening, a friend will come to the shop. You will know him when he says your name. Be careful!

The letter surprised and pleased Johanna. Now she felt ready for an adventure. She hid the letter when Mr Todd arrived at the entrance to the shop.

'Hot water, Charley!' the barber shouted. 'I can see a customer coming. It's old Mr Wrankley. He owns the newspaper shop at the end of Fleet Street. Good afternoon, Mr Wrankley. A shave for you? Charley, hand me the razor.'

As she was passing the razor to Mr Todd, Johanna had a little accident. She made a small cut on one arm of the barber's chair.

'Boy! What have you done? You've hurt a very good razor. Get me a different one. Is there any news in the town, Mr Wrankley?'

'Do you know Mr Cummings, the carriage driver? He's been terribly sick since twelve o'clock last night. He says, "Oh, those pies, those pies!" all the time.'

'Very strange,' replied the barber.

'Well, he's not the most intelligent man around here. Perhaps the problem's in his head and not in his stomach.'

'Did you visit him on your way here?' asked Todd.

'No, sir, I left home quite secretly. My wife's cousin, Mr John Mundel, came to the house last night. He had a wonderful pearl necklace with him. He asked me to take it to some of the jewellery shops near the palace. I'm going to ask them if it's valuable. Mundel thinks it belongs to the queen. He wants twelve thousand pounds for it. I didn't tell my wife, but I want to sell it for her cousin. She thinks I've gone north on newspaper business. I've got the necklace here in my pocket.'

'How interesting! Now, I'll shave you again so you'll look your best. Charley, go to Mr Cummings's house and ask about his health. There's no need to hurry.'

◆

When Johanna returned from her visit to Mr Cummings, Mr Wrankley was gone. Sweeney Todd was cleaning his razors.

'Well, Charley,' the barber said, 'how is Mr Cummings?'

'His wife says he's better. He was sleeping.'

'Oh, very good. I must look at some papers in my sitting-room. I don't want any customers for the next ten minutes. If somebody comes to the door, I'm not here.'

Johanna heard the key turn in the sitting-room lock. She felt afraid, but she walked as silently as possible to the cupboard. The door wasn't completely closed and she looked inside. On the first shelf was Mr Wrankley's hat. 'What's happened?' the girl thought nervously. She reached for the barber's chair so she didn't fall. She looked at the arm of the chair and remembered the small cut from that morning. But the arm was perfect, with no cuts or burns. It was the same chair as this morning, but the arm was different.

'I can't explain this,' thought Johanna. 'Am I in a dream?' She covered her face with her hands. When she looked up again, Sweeney Todd was watching her.

Johanna thought quickly and screamed loudly in pain.

'What's the meaning of this?' growled Sweeney Todd. 'What were you doing out here? Something must be done about you.'

'Yes, sir. You're right. I'm going to go to the dentist's tomorrow. My tooth has ached all day. I'm sorry that it's worried you.'

Was this excuse true or not? Todd wasn't sure. 'You'll be better tomorrow,' he said to Johanna. 'Watch the shop. I'm going back to my sitting-room.'

When he was alone, Sweeney Todd took the pearl necklace from his pocket.

'My fortune continues to grow! John Mundel has lost his money and the necklace. I'll sell it in Belgium. But before I leave England, I must kill Mrs Lovett. She's not part of my plan, and I won't give her any of my money.'

He took the small packet of poison from his pocket and smiled at it. Then he put it back in his pocket and returned to the shop.

'I'm going out,' the barber told Johanna. 'I'll return in one hour and not more. Watch the shop carefully and I'll pay you well.'

Johanna wanted to search the shop, but she had no time. A carriage arrived outside and a man hurried in. He was a tall, handsome man and he spoke politely to the girl. 'Don't be frightened, Miss Oakley. I know your friend Mr Jeffery. I sent a letter to you this morning. We must hurry. Is there a hiding place in the shop?'

'Yes,' said Johanna. 'The cupboard is very big.'

The tall man hurried to the entrance and called to his two officers. They climbed into the cupboard and the other man closed the door.

'When the barber returns, I'll come in for a shave. Tonight we'll discover everything about Mr Todd. Perhaps something about Mark Ingestrie too.'

'Sir, you're so kind. Who are you?' Johanna asked.

'I'm a judge – Sir Richard Blunt. I'll help you as much as I can.'

'But, sir, please be careful. There's something dangerous about that chair. Please don't sit in it,' Johanna said.

'I think I know the mystery. Now I have to prove it, but don't worry about me. I'll leave now – Todd mustn't find me here. Remember, Johanna: you're not alone.'

◆

At that minute, Sweeney Todd was on his way to Bell Court. When he went into Mrs Lovett's pie shop, he greeted the owner with a pleasant smile on his ugly face. Mrs Lovett was waiting for the nine o'clock tray of pies to come up from the cellar. This was the second busiest time of day for her.

'Good evening, Mr Todd. Will you come into my sitting-room, sir?' invited Mrs Lovett.

The barber and Mrs Lovett sat down together for quite a serious conversation.
'Mr Todd, when is this business going to end? These pies are giving me bad dreams at night. And the new pie man is already a problem. You have to do something about him.'

'Mrs Lovett, please be calm. Everything is going to be fine for both of us. Would you like a drink? Can I get you a glass of your favourite wine? Where do you keep it?'

'There's a bottle in the cupboard behind me,' said Mrs Lovett. 'Thank you. I need a glass of something before I see the next tray of pies.'

Mr Todd turned his back on Mrs Lovett and poured a large glass of wine for her. He took the poison from his pocket and added it to the wine. Then he gave the glass to Mrs Lovett. 'My dear lady, I've got good news for you. I'm ready to shut my shop and leave London. I'll count our money and give you your part tomorrow evening. There will be more than twenty thousand pounds for you from our eight years of business together. Will that stop your bad dreams?'

'Wonderful!' cried Mrs Lovett. 'I'll leave too, but we must live in different countries. I don't want any trouble from the police, and I don't want to see you ever again. But don't forget about the pie man. I think he's dangerous.'

'I'll return at midnight and look after him too,' Todd said.

Mrs Lovett finished her glass of wine. She and the barber went back into the shop as a woman came through the door.

'Would you like a cold pie, madam? The hot pies will be ready at nine o'clock.'

'No thank you, Mrs Lovett. You don't know me, but my name is Mrs Wrankley. My husband owns the newspaper shop at the end of Fleet Street. Can you put one of these signs in your window for me?'

'What's this about?' asked Mrs Lovett.

Mrs Wrankley's tears began to fall. 'My husband's missing. He left home carrying a valuable piece of jewellery. He wanted to sell a pearl necklace, but he's disappeared. His description is on the signs. I can't eat or sleep.'

'Try one of these delicious pies,' suggested Sweeney Todd with a wicked look on his face. 'One bite and you'll soon see *something* of Mr Wrankley.'

The woman didn't know what to do. She bit into the pie and seemed to feel better. 'I'll hope for the best,' she said, leaving the shop.

◆

In Mrs Lovett's cellar Jarvis Williams woke up at six o'clock in the afternoon after a good long sleep. Both his body and his mind were well rested.

'I've got three hours before the next tray of pies is needed. There's some mystery in this place and I'm going to discover it. But more important, I'm going to find a way out of this terrible prison.'

The small window above opened and Mrs Lovett shouted at her pie maker. 'Listen, Mr Williams. I'll need two trays of pies tonight, not the usual one tray. Have them ready at exactly nine o'clock.'

'Mrs Lovett, this is too much. I don't want to make any more pies.'

'Be careful, young man. You're going to make trouble for yourself,' Mrs Lovett said mysteriously. 'You can leave tomorrow morning after I find a new pie man. Tonight, make two trays of pies for me. Then we'll shake hands in the morning and you can go.'

Jarvis Williams needed some time because he had a plan. 'You're very kind, Mrs Lovett, so I agree. I'll send two trays of pies up to the shop at nine o'clock.'

Mrs Lovett closed the window above Mr Williams and the cellar was silent again.

'I can't believe anything she says,' thought Jarvis Williams. 'I must find a way out of here.' He looked around the cellar and tried to think. Finally he noticed the tools that he used for pie making. 'Why haven't I thought of those before? I can break doors and windows with them.'

The young man began his search behind the meat shelves. 'There has to be a door or window back here. Every morning there's plenty of fresh meat on the shelves.'

With his tools Williams pulled one of the shelves off the wall. He couldn't see a door, but he felt the wall carefully. Finally he found something. He could feel the four sides of a door. He hit this part of the wall very hard with his heaviest tool and a small door opened in front of him. Williams looked through the door and saw darkness behind it.

'Now I know how the meat arrives on the shelves. But what part of Mrs Lovett's house does it come from? I'll go through the door and find out.'

With a light from the main part of the cellar, he went through the door behind the meat shelves. When he could see inside the next room, he screamed. He hurried back into the main part of the cellar and lay on the floor for about fifteen minutes.

'Is it true? Have I really seen such terrible things? Was I dreaming or is it possible?' But then he looked around and saw the broken shelf and the open door. He sat down on the little chair near the ovens and tried to think.

The window above him opened again. 'It's eight o'clock, Mr Williams, and I can't hear the ovens. Will my pies be ready at nine?'

'Don't worry, madam. You'll have them on time.'

'Good,' said Mrs Lovett. 'I'm glad that you're being sensible.' She closed the window and smiled. 'Sweeney Todd has a plan for you tonight, my dear pie man.'

Jarvis Williams started making the pies. He had a plan too, but Mrs Lovett must not know about it. 'I'll make her pies,' the young man thought. 'But I've got a surprise for her at nine o'clock. Something as terrible as her pies!'

Johanna was alone in the barber's shop except, of course, for the two officers hidden in the cupboard. She sat and thought about Mark Ingestrie.

'Where are you, Mark? What happened to our plans?' She began to cry and tears ran down her pretty face. 'I mustn't look sad. I'm the barber's boy and must act the part.' She stood up and began to sweep the floor. Soon Todd returned.

'Has anybody been in?' he growled at Johanna.

'Yes, sir. A man came in and asked for a shave.'

'Shut the door and lock it. You can sleep here on the floor. I don't want any more customers tonight. You haven't looked into my private things, have you?'

'No, sir. Of course not.'

Todd walked towards the cupboard. He started to open it, but a man walked through the entrance into the shop.

'Good evening, barber,' said the man. 'I'd like a clean shave, please.'

'It's quite late. Come back in the morning.'

'But sir, I must go back to my farm in Braintree tomorrow morning. I've finished my business in London. I sold all the animals that I brought with me – two hundred and twenty of them – and for a very good price. One more night in the Bull's Head Hotel and then I'll go home with a pocket full of money. I'd like to go home with a clean face too. My wife, and my daughter Johanna, will be very happy tomorrow when I arrive.'

Johanna! Suddenly the girl knew that the customer was the judge in farmer's clothes.

'Charley, bring me some hot water!' shouted the barber. 'And then, while I'm finishing this customer, go to Mrs Lovett's pie shop. Have a pie and don't hurry. We'll close after I've finished with this customer.'

Johanna walked out but hid next to the door of the shop.

'Did the man at the Bull's Head tell you about my shop?' Todd asked the man.

'No, I thought of a shave when I saw your sign. I didn't know there was a barber's shop in this area.'

'And did you travel to London alone?' asked Todd.

'Oh, yes. I always do business alone.'

'Very wise. Very wise. Sir, your beard is quite heavy. I need a stronger razor. I'll get one from the other room. Then you'll get a very clean shave. I'll be back in one minute, sir. Sit there and be comfortable.'

Sweeney Todd went into his sitting-room, taking the light with him. When the barber was out of the room the customer, Sir Richard Blunt, quickly and silently jumped out of the chair. He stood in a dark corner and waited.

In about ten seconds, a terribly loud noise came from the sitting-room. Then

suddenly, the barber's chair turned over and disappeared below the floor. Another chair then mysteriously took the place of the first chair. Everything in the room *looked* the same, but this was a different chair.

So this explained how Sweeney Todd's rich customers disappeared! But what really happened to them? The chair turned and they fell ten metres to a stone floor below the shop. They died when their heads hit the floor. Then Sweeney Todd robbed them, taking everything valuable. And finally, *they were cut up for Mrs Lovett's pies!*

But this time was different. Sir Richard Blunt now hurried out of his corner and sat down in the new chair. He made himself comfortable and waited. In another minute the barber returned to his shop with the light.

'I hope that's the last one,' Todd said to himself. 'For some reason, I felt nervous this time. That's never happened before. And he was so quiet! They usually produce a good scream. I didn't even hear the body hit the floor below.'

Then the barber saw Sir Richard sitting calmly in the chair with shaving soap on his face. The cry that came from Sweeney Todd's mouth was terrible.

'Sir, what's the matter?' asked Sir Richard.

'No!' cried Todd. 'Don't look at me with your dead eyes!'

'Murderer!' shouted Sir Richard. He jumped up and held Sweeney Todd by his neck. The two officers came out of the cupboard.

'Take him away,' ordered Sir Richard. 'Miss Oakley, this is the murderer. I discovered his secret chair last night when I was in the cellars of St Dunstan's Church. His wicked activities will stop now.'

◆

It was five minutes before nine o'clock and Mrs Lovett's pie shop in Bell Court was crowded with hungry customers. Finally the crowd heard the clock at St Dunstan's. They knew it was time for a delicious pie.

'I can hear the lift,' shouted Mrs Lovett. 'The first tray of pies is coming.'

The lift opened and a large tray, about two metres square, came into view. But what was happening? The pies started to move. They were falling off the tray.

Suddenly a man jumped off the tray and into the shop.

Mrs Lovett screamed when she saw Jarvis Williams. Everybody in the shop was silent. Then Mr Williams spoke. 'Dear customers, I'm afraid I'm going to destroy your happy evening. But it's always good to have the facts. Mrs Lovett's pies are not made from the usual sort of meat. They're made from Mr Sweeney Todd's customers.'

Some people were sick immediately. Others ran out of the shop and hurried home. Nobody wanted to believe Mr Williams – but nobody wanted to eat another one of Mrs Lovett's pies.

'No, it's not true,' screamed Mrs Lovett.

'I think the judge will decide that, madam. I'm here to take you to prison,' said a policeman. 'You and Mr Sweeney Todd have murdered many people.'

Mrs Lovett sat down suddenly. Her face was very red. 'But ... Oh! Somebody has given me poison. It was Todd, I'm sure of it.' Then she fell to the floor – dead.

At the entrance to the pie shop there was now a different and much smaller crowd of people: Sir Richard Blunt, Mr Jeffery, Johanna Oakley and Tobias Ragg.

'Miss Oakley, I want to introduce you to somebody,' said Sir Richard. 'I found him last night in Mrs Lovett's cellar. We planned this surprise for Mrs Lovett together. Here he is, the pie man.'

'Mark – Mark Ingestrie!' screamed Johanna. 'You aren't dead!'

'No, I never was. And you, Johanna, aren't in love with another man. I saw you with Mr Jeffery in Temple Gardens. I thought that he was your new sweetheart.'

◆

What did the future hold for these people? Sweeney Todd was hanged. Mr Fogg's Special Hospital was closed, and he was sent to prison. Tobias and his mother got jobs working for Mark Ingestrie and his wife, Johanna. The police took the heads of Todd's dead customers from the cellars under St Dunstan's, and people began to go to church there again. They didn't know why the terrible smell disappeared. The police decided not to explain everything.

Johanna and Mark lived happily together. Mark sometimes talked about his adventures in India. But more often he looked at the stars and felt grateful: for his escape from Mrs Lovett's cellar, for his good friend, poor Mr Thornhill, for his wife and young family, and for the pearl necklace.

Sweeney Todd as a TV murder mystery

1 Discuss these questions in groups of six.

a Why should people watch a TV programme about Sweeney Todd, in your opinion?

b How will the time, the place and the people in the story make it interesting?

c Would you like to watch this programme? Why (not)?

2 Continue working in your group. Discuss the reasons why these are important to the story.

a an unusually loud noise that often comes from the barber's shop

b a valuable pearl necklace

c Mrs Lovett's delicious meat pies

d Mr King's small silver box

e hats, walking-sticks, umbrellas and jewellery in Sweeney Todd's cupboards

f the bad smell in St Dunstan's Church

g poison from the chemist's shop

h a cut in one arm of the barber's chair

3 Discuss the part of the TV programme when Sweeney Todd is in court.

a Which people from the story will answer questions in court? Make a list.

b What questions will the judge ask Sweeney Todd and the other people?

4 Act out this part of the story. Prove that Sweeney Todd is *not* innocent.

Sweeney Todd was hanged for murder. Everyone in London followed the barber's terrible story in the newspapers. You are a young newspaper writer looking for your first big story. You are interested in the people who knew Sweeney Todd. Choose someone from the book and write his or her story.

1 Write your questions for this person.

2 Think of a title that will interest your readers. Then write your newspaper story.

1 Read about fast food. Then discuss the questions below with two or three other students.

Fast food for busy lives

Two thousand years ago, in Roman cities, many people left their flats for a quick breakfast. Later in the day they could eat cooked meat and fish in special shops called *popinae*. Now, all over the world, people buy fast food from restaurants and street sellers. They eat it there or take it home. Everyone knows the big names like McDonald's and Burger King, but small cafés in every town sell fast food too.

In London, in the 1700s and 1800s, working class people enjoyed buying cooked pies from pie shops. These were made with cheap bits of meat, and were often eaten with potato. On the coasts people bought their potatoes with fish; this is still many Britons' favourite fast food. Sandwiches also became popular in the 1700s. The Earl of Sandwich did not want to stop work for lunch, so he ate dried meat in bread. Now, of course, Britons enjoy fast food dishes from around the world.

a   Do you like fast food? Can you buy any near your home?

b   How many reasons can you think of for the popularity of fast food?

c   How often do you eat fast food for lunch?

d   What is the most popular lunch-time food in your country? Is it different for different age groups?

2 Write the names of popular foods from different countries in your notebooks. How many countries' dishes can you name? How many of these foods have you tried?

3 **Work with two or three other students. You want to open a lunch-time café. Discuss what is important for its success. Put these ideas in order from most (1) to least (13) important. Add your own ideas to the list.**

☐ Size of meals   ☐ Position in the town

☐ Cost   ☐ Friendly welcome

☐ Smell   ☐ Speed

☐ Comfort   ☐ Big menu

☐ Health   ☐ Size of café

☐ Type of food   ☐ Good cooks/waiters/cleaners

☐ Opening hours   ....

....

4 **Write a list of questions to ask possible customers. Then ask ten or more students to answer your questions. Note down their opinions.**

5 **Plan and write about your café with your group.**

a   Think of a name for your lunch-time café. Write this at the top of your menu.

b   Think about the food and the look of the menu. Then write the menu.

c   Prepare a short advertisement (50 words or fewer) about your new café
for the radio.

Menu

For the radio: